COLLINS GEM
ANTIQUE MARKS

a mine of information

GW00372992

COLLINS GEM
CRICKET

a mine of information

COLLINS GEM
DIETING
FAT

a mine of information

COLLINS GEM
DOGS

a mine of information

COLLINS GEM
FIRST AID

a mine of information

Connect

COLLINS GEM
PREDICTION

a mine of information

COLLINS GEM
Ready
REFERENCE

a mine of information

COLLINS GEM
SHARKS

a mine of information

COLLINS GEM
WHALES
& DOLPHINS

a mine of information

COLLINS GEM
WHISKY

a mine of information

COLLINS GEM
WORD
PROCESSING

a mine of information

COLLINS GEM
Your PC

a mine of information

COLLINS GEM

Creating
WEB PAGES

Alex Gray

HarperCollins*Publishers*

Alex Gray managed network systems and computer services for the BBC's Open University Production Centre for over ten years, and has been editor of *Corel User* magazine since 1996. Alex is now Technical Director of Wordworks Ltd, which provides technical authoring, training, magazine production and website design services, and is also the author of *Collins Gem Internet*.
He can be contacted at: alex.gray@mail.com

HarperCollins*Publishers*
Westerhill Road, Bishopbriggs, Glasgow G64 2QT

First published 2000

Reprint 10 9 8 7 6 5 4 3 2 1 0

ISBN 0 00 472477 1

Printed in Italy by Amadeus S.p.A.

Contents

Words in bold are cross references to other sections or to words in the glossary, or indicate computer commands, depending on the context.

Preface

Everywhere, there are references to websites – on posters, adverts, TV and radio programmes; everything from bus tickets to jet aircraft. These are constant reminders of the vast web of corporate and commercial sites out on the Internet – sites that have probably had thousands of pounds spent on designing, building, maintaining and promoting them.

And countless academic and official sites provide all manner of other useful and valuable information.

But what about you and your information? Wouldn't it be great if you could tell the world all about your locality, your interests, your club, or even just publish a family newsletter for friends and relatives around the world? Well, the good news is that you can, and the really good news is that it certainly won't cost you thousands of pounds or take years of computer study!

Collins Gem Creating Web Pages shows you how to be a home-based, worldwide, round-the-clock publisher, thanks to the power of the Internet, and using nothing more than a regular home PC, a telephone connection and free Internet software.

Your message might be something of interest to only a handful of friends and relatives, or it might bring you recognition and thanks from around the world. Either way you'll experience the thrill of seeing your own words and pictures instantly published worldwide. Now read on, and make it happen!

INTRODUCTION

What is the World Wide Web?

Like many great innovations, the World Wide Web, or just 'Web' for short, has grown out of a simple idea that occurred in the right place at the right time. In 1990, Tim Berners-Lee, working at CERN in Geneva, worked out how to link the research laboratory's mountains of computer-based research papers in a useful way. His key idea was to provide a way to mark certain words as '**hyperlinks**', which would jump automatically on-screen to related documents.

CERN staff set about turning this idea into a reality. They developed a computer program – the **browser** – for viewing and navigating these linked documents. At the same time, the public computer network was expanding at an ever-increasing rate, interconnecting existing computer networks and terminals around the world and forming the **Internet**.

After a few documents are linked to other documents, which are in turn linked to yet more documents, maybe including a link back to the original one, you will have a computerized 'web' of linked documents. If you add in a way to create links to documents on other computers across a **network**, and connect this up to the Internet,

Read all about the origins of the Web on the CERN website at www.cern.ch/public

you now have a worldwide web of interconnected document collections. This is the **World Wide Web**.

Although the Web was originally designed just for plain text documents and simple diagrams, it has been rapidly enhanced to encompass all manner of graphics and other snazzy content, and in a decade has become what some regard as the greatest development in publishing technology since metal type.

With just a few mouse clicks, documents from any corner of the world can be delivered directly to your computer screen, and you can instantly follow links to related materials, even though these may be on different computers that are located thousands of miles away from each other. And all for the cost of a local phone call.

The World Wide Web is a great resource for someone looking for information or entertainment, and for companies keen to promote their products and services. But unlike traditional print and broadcasting media, the Web also offers terrific advantages for the would-be self-publisher:

Low cost   Web publishing costs are very much lower than for traditional paper publishing, and you don't need to make expensive guesses as to what the demand for your publication will be. Once your website is published, it costs you no more for 10,000 people to view it than it does for 10. Better still, if you already have a PC and **modem**, you can get a worthwhile website online for a cash cost of only a few pennies.

Accessibility   For many people, this is the key feature of Internet publishing – you can publish your information around the world moments after you have written it on your own PC. Occasionally this can lead to problems if you haven't been careful in what you say! But, of course, even after you have published your material, you can update it easily and as frequently as you like.

Availability Your website will be available 24 hours a day around the globe at no extra cost to you – your own computer doesn't need to be online except for the brief periods when you are actually publishing new or updated material (*see* **Going live**, *page 117*). This is particularly important if you want people overseas in other time zones to benefit from your website.

Flexibility Web pages can make very effective use of different type styles, colouring and sophisticated layouts. But beyond attractive layout of text and pictures, web pages can also present a range of dynamic materials that are simply not feasible to publish in print. These include sound and video material, animated diagrams and pictures that can be zoomed in and out or panned around by the viewer. (*See* **Putting on the style**, *page 136*)

Why have a website?

Since you are reading this book, it's a fair guess that you probably have an idea of what you want a website for. If you have already browsed around a wide selection of websites, the chances are that you will already be buzzing with ideas for a website of your own.

If you haven't yet browsed the Internet to see what's on offer, start right now! All the equipment you need for browsing the Web (basically a PC with a modem and some free software) will also be needed for creating and checking your own web pages, so get that set up as soon as possible (*see* **Before you begin**, *page 14*).

Use your browser's **favorites** (or **bookmarks**) facility to keep a note of any sites that might inspire your own designs later. While it wouldn't be proper to copy their content wholesale, many sites will use elements of design that you like and can readily adapt. But be realistic – some of the best sites will have been created by teams of highly-paid professionals who do this day-in, day-out, and you can't expect to match their best efforts on your first foray into website design!

While browsing, you may notice that most websites seem to fall into one of three categories: sites just for fun and entertainment, sites for business and commercial purposes, and sites intended to impart very particular information. But of course many of the best sites provide a compelling combination of all three.

For fun   You might want to create a fun site to entertain and stimulate others with similar interests or in a similar situation. It could be some sort of online club room for other people of your age or occupation, an entertaining diary of life in your school or locality, or just a collection of your favourite jokes and puzzles. Fun sites often include a **guest book** where your visitors can leave a little information about themselves and say what they think of your site.

For business   Do you work in a business that would benefit from promotion on the Internet? You can publicize your products and services to new customers, or provide after-sales service or new product information to keep existing customers in touch. Full-blown commercial sales systems are beyond the scope of this book, but what you will learn here will provide an excellent grounding if you have considered developing or commissioning more advanced e-commerce systems.

To inform   You might have a collection of useful niche information that you would like to share with the world. On a website you can present your information attractively and flexibly, with links to related sites and other sources. Some very successful commercial websites have started out from someone's desire just to publish information they have collected and organized for the benefit of a wider audience. Topics on existing websites range from train-spotting to turbo-engine tuning, and bee-keeping to book-keeping, but you may well have a new insight or special collection of information even on an existing topic.

Although you may, for
example, adopt an overall
informational style, your site will probably contain
elements of at least two of the above categories. For
instance, your local town information site might be
livened up with a few local myths or a puzzle to solve
based on facts found in the site, or it might promote
some of the local businesses.

Whatever your topic, once your information is published
on the Internet, you will probably find people from all
around the world offering additional facts, extra resources
such as pictures, **links** to related websites, or ideas for new
topics. And, in the course of preparing and presenting
material for your own site, you could well come across all
manner of other sites of great interest on similar topics.
And if you don't, well then you will have the satisfaction of
knowing what a unique website you are creating!

You can do it!

For anyone who hasn't done it before, publishing material on the Web can seem a daunting black art, but it really isn't difficult and anyone capable of using a word processor on a PC should have no trouble producing a basic website. Of course, it helps if you have some flair for presentation and layout, but even if you don't, there are plenty of template systems that will generate a respectable looking page populated with your own words and pictures (*see* **Authoring tools**, *page 36*).

Whatever your eventual purpose, this book will tell you what you need to know to get started on the stimulating and satisfying road to World Wide Web publishing. And it takes a lot to beat the feeling of achievement and pride you will get from seeing your own creation published to the world!

BEFORE YOU BEGIN

The good news is that to create a website of your own you really need nothing more than a computer running a simple text editor, so almost any regular PC or Mac computer is up to the task. In practice, your computer must be able to run a modern **browser** (such as *Microsoft Internet Explorer* or *Netscape Navigator*) so you can view the results of your handiwork. Almost all modern home computers are supplied already kitted out for this purpose. You are likely to want to run more sophisticated web design programs, known as **authoring tools** (*see* **Tools of the trade**, *page 29*), but even these programs generally make modest demands on modern PCs.

You can create a website on your own computer and view it directly from your own hard disk, but to get the most out of your website work you will also want to be able to **upload** it to a **host** computer on the Internet so that anyone around the world can access it from the World Wide Web. For this you will need an Internet connection, and on a home computer this is achieved using a **modem** to connect your computer via a telephone line to an **Internet Service Provider** (*see* **Getting connected**, *page 16*). The company you use as a service provider need not be the same company that hosts your website, but often it will be (*see* **Finding a host**, *page 22*).

If you cannot have your own Internet connection, perhaps because you have no phone line available, it is perfectly possible to give the files (on a floppy disk, for example) to someone else with a connection who can do the uploading for you. You might also do this if you have a lot of material to upload and have a fast direct connection available elsewhere, such as at a college.

GETTING THE HARDWARE

Almost any home PC bought in the last few years is more than capable of handling basic web authoring work. If you already have a computer set up to browse the Web, then you already have all the essentials for basic website creation. However, if you are buying a new machine and you expect to progress to advanced web creation software, you should check out the software's hardware requirements just in case it warrants a higher computer specification. You might also want a more powerful computer with plenty of disk space if you intend to do a lot of image manipulation or multimedia work for your website (*see* **Putting on the style**, *page 136*).

Most home computers are supplied with an internal modem and Internet access software as standard. If yours doesn't have one, you can purchase a modem for £50–£100, depending on features and quality. Ideally, get a modem conforming to the V.90 specification, which will give you the speediest connection possible on a good ordinary telephone line.

If you expect to spend a lot of time online, or you need a second phone line for computer use, you should also consider a digital telephone line (**ISDN**) such as British

Telecom's *Home Highway*, which can provide faster, more reliable Internet connections. This needs a special form of modem called a terminal adaptor and may cost more to install than a simple phone line, but it can carry two calls at once and could pay for itself in shorter call times and the convenience of a dedicated line.

There is more information on equipping yourself for Internet access in the *Collins Gem Internet* book, and up-to-date computer reviews and prices are available in a wide range of computer magazines and websites.

OTHER EQUIPMENT

You will find a CD-ROM drive almost essential, as this is the way that most software is supplied nowadays, and pretty well all home PCs include these drives as a standard fitting. If you intend to use the Web to present original artwork or photos, you may also need to invest in a basic scanner or digital camera, and for a really adventurous site you might get a camera suitable for use as a webcam (*see* **Putting on the style**, *page 136*). Digital cameras transfer their pictures directly to your computer and can save a lot of time and processing costs. All these extras can be as fancy and expensive as you want, but the cheaper models are generally adequate for web work.

GETTING CONNECTED

If you already have a computer set up to browse the Internet, then you are more or less home and dry. Your existing connection and account should automatically support any other Internet software you may decide to use, for example to upload your web pages (*see* **Going live**, *page 117*).

If you don't have a connection, you will need to make arrangements with a **service provider** (*see below*), and you must set up Internet dial-up connection software on your computer. For simplicity, the following details assume you are using a PC-compatible computer, but similar procedures apply to the Apple Macintosh range.

SERVICE PROVIDERS

To connect your computer modem to the Internet, you need an account with some sort of **Internet Access Provider** or **Internet Service Provider** (usually abbreviated to **ISP**). As the name suggests, an access provider makes just the basic connection to the Internet and it is up to you to obtain any other services you want to use. A full service provider (**ISP**) offers additional services such as storing your e-mail until you go online to retrieve it, and perhaps offering you some website storage space as part of your account.

The range of services on offer, and their costs, vary widely from supplier to supplier. Many accounts are free except for local phone call charges while you are online (the provider receives a share of the phone revenue). For simplicity, we will use the term **service provider** to cover all the various flavours of dial-up connection services. The most popular service providers in the UK include BT, Freeserve, Tesco,

Virgin, Which?, AOL, CompuServe and Demon, but there are many others.

To keep costs down, choose a service provider that offers local telephone dialling from your area. Most providers offer special numbers for local rate calls from anywhere in the UK. The actual cost of 'local rate' depends on who provides your telephone services, so if you find you are spending a lot of time online you might want to shop around on this front as well (*see* **Cutting the cost**, *opposite*).

Some Internet magazines provide up-to-date listings of ISPs, their charges and quality of service (from independent surveys). It is by no means true to say that you will always get better service from a paid provider than from a free one, or that a dearer provider will offer better service than a cheap one.

SETTING UP A SERVICE

To start using a service provider you need Internet access software on your computer, configured to connect with your chosen provider. The easiest way to set this up for major service providers is to use the free CD-ROMs available from magazine inserts, direct mailshots, or the providers' customer service departments (their details can be found in magazines, in adverts, or on the Web itself). CD-ROMs for the ISPs operated on behalf of large store chains such as Tesco or Virgin are usually available from the company stores. The CD-ROMs automate the complete procedure of installing the software, configuring it for a particular

CUTTING THE COST

If you spend a lot of time online, it is worth finding out which telecom company (for example, Cable & Wireless, MCI or Telinco) provides the 0845 service to your ISP. Then check to see if that telecom provider also offers reduced calling rates for 'indirect access' calls routed over their lines. Although these services are usually sold for cheaper long-distance calls, many offer an extra discount for local-rate calls that end up on their own lines.

If you make frequent short connections (for example, to check e-mail), then also check which providers have the lowest minimum call charges and by-the-second rates, as this could also save you a lot.

The indirect routes are usually accessed from BT lines by dialling a prefix before the number (for example, 132 for C&W, 166 for MCI, 1401 for Telinco). You don't need to leave BT to use these services and the savings can be substantial, especially during peak hours when BT is at its most expensive.

provider, and signing-up to obtain an account name and password. Setting up your system should be simply a matter of loading the CD-ROM and following the automated prompts.

The installation will usually customize your system to give first preference to the ISP who provided the disk, and will brand your browser to their company name and logo. If you want to

add a new provider to your system without removing an existing one, it may be better to ask for instructions on configuring your system manually. This is usually no more difficult than clicking the **New Connection** icon in your **Dial-up Networking** settings, and entering details supplied by the service provider. Most providers make the instructions available online, and you can retrieve and print these using your existing connection before setting up a new one.

The minimum you need to set up a new connection is the provider's dial-up phone number. If you want to use the new provider to handle e-mail as well, you will need server addresses for incoming and outgoing mail. When you dial up, you will need an account name and password to log on to the service. There may be standard access codes for the first log on of all new subscribers, and you will register unique details during your first session. In other cases, especially with paid-for service providers, you may need to call the provider to obtain details in advance. Some set-ups provide a very useful reference page of your account details for you to print out for future reference.

Most ISP's CD-ROMs will install and configure Microsoft's *Internet Explorer* for you, and for

STAYING UP TO DATE

The Web is developing very quickly, and browsers are being updated all the time. Some updates are completely new versions, but most are minor revisions (sometimes called **service packs**) or extra **components** to handle new features. If your computer came with *Internet Explorer* pre-installed, or if you installed it from an old free CD-ROM, you probably won't have the latest version on your system, but once you have your basic Internet connection set up you can obtain all the latest components online.

If you point your *Internet Explorer* browser to `www.microsoft.com/windows/ie/download`, the web server will run an automatic check on your system and present you with a status report on your browser setup. If you want to install any new components or to update your existing software, you can download just the required parts and have them installed automatically.

If your download is interrupted, the system can also save it and resume from the same point later. This is a superb facility, but some of the downloads are very large, especially for a completely new version, and it might be better to obtain a more recent CD-ROM instead.

convenience in this book we will assume you are using this on a PC computer running Windows. Very handily, the free disks usually also include Microsoft *FrontPage Express*, which is a web authoring tool that we will use as an example later (*see* **Authoring tools**, *page 36*). However, pretty well everything in the book has direct equivalents in *Netscape Communicator*, which includes *Netscape Composer* for web page creation and is particularly popular on the Apple Macintosh.

FINDING A HOST

To have a website permanently available on the Internet, you need to use an Internet **web server** (or host) that will accept files from you, store them, and make them available on demand. In the early days of the Web this was something that could cost a lot, usually as a monthly charge of several pounds per megabyte, but there are now all sorts of free or low-cost options that can provide all you need for a modest home-grown website.

The easiest option is usually the web server space that service providers commonly include with their access accounts. If your main interest in having an Internet account is to create web pages, the amount of server space on offer may be a key factor in your choice of service provider.

Remember, many service providers are free and there is no reason why you shouldn't have more than one account, perhaps one that suits you best for connection and another for free web space. You don't have to pay anything when you are not online, but read the small print, because some free providers require you to log on every so often, maybe once a month, to keep your account active. Some allow you to upload fresh web pages only while connected to the Internet through their own dial-up service.

The free web space on offer may seem quite small in comparison to the size of your hard disk, just a few megabytes (MB), but for ordinary web pages a few MB is quite a lot of space. Many pages will need no more than a few kilobytes (KB) for a simple design, so 1 MB of server space could potentially hold dozens of web pages. Pictures can take much more storage and files for downloading could be megabytes each, so how much space you need depends very much on the nature of your site (*see* **Planning your website**, *page 47*).

If you want to create a large site you may need to pay for space, and you should shop around. Bear in mind that your web server could be anywhere in the world – some of the best deals are available in the USA and the Far East. The sample site developed later in this book happened to be hosted in Singapore!

WHAT'S YOUR ADDRESS?

As you probably know from your own browsing, every web page has a unique 'address' known as its **URL** (which stands for Uniform Resource Locator). URLs conform to a worldwide standard, and the main parts are a **domain name**, identifying the host server, and more detailed file information identifying the specific page on the server (*see* **Anatomy of a URL**, *page 24*).

ANATOMY OF A URL

```
http://www.gairloch.co.uk/
collins-gem/welcome.htm
```

A typical URL such as this is made up of several distinct parts to identify a file anywhere on the Internet. The first part, before the www, just indicates what method is to be used to retrieve the file, and **http** (hypertext transfer protocol) is the standard method used for all regular web pages. For speed when entering a URL, you can usually omit this first part and the browser will assume it is http://. You may also come across **ftp** (file transfer protocol), used to transfer files directly between the server and your disk drive.

The next part, up to the first single oblique stroke /, is the **domain name** of the Internet-connected computer that holds the required file. Special computers, known as **domain name servers**, provide the information needed to route your request to the named computer, wherever it is in the world. If you are connecting to the main **home page** of a website, there may be no more details needed after the domain name and you will be connected to a suitable starting page on the site.

If you are looking for a specific page, such as welcome.htm, in a specific directory, such as collins-gem, then these names will follow the domain name separated by oblique strokes in much the same way as may be familiar to you from your own PC's filing system. Pages intended for direct access will usually be kept in fairly simple locations, with clickable links to the more obscure pages within the site (*see* **Structural design**, *page 59*).

Given the hundreds of millions of pages out on the Web, these elements are clearly vital when you are looking for a particular piece of information. You simply type the URL into your browser and the request is passed to the appropriate computer anywhere in the world, which sends back the page for display.

If you are using web space provided free by your service provider, your domain name will usually be derived from the ISP's name. On paid-for services your domain name may be a prefix on the provider's name. For example, on Demon Internet it might be www.collins-gem.demon.co.uk. On a free web page service it is more likely to be an extension on the end of the provider's domain name, for example members.tripod.co.uk/CollinsGEM.

On free web space systems such as the popular *Geocities* (*see* **Tools of the trade**, *page 29*), your URL might be something like www.geocities.com/ Athens/Delphi/9312/CollinsGEM. These names can be cumbersome to type or memorize, and you may feel they present a bad image. The proper way to avoid them is to register a full domain name of your own, such as `collins-gem.com`, but this will involve some expense and formality (*see* **Registering a domain name**, *opposite*). Once you have registered your own name you are free to organize your site as you wish, and to tag on whatever sub-names you want after the domain name (*see* **Planning your server structure**, *page 68*).

An alternative, free, solution is to register with a **URL redirection service**. These services offer more memorable names – such as `welcome.to/collins-gem` – and a clever system that redirects browsers automatically (and usually invisibly) to another site, possibly your free site with the long-winded name. In this particular example, your URL is actually located in the domain of Tonga (`.to`)! These services are usually funded by a small additional advertising window that pops up when a visitor is redirected, or a small advertising banner on your first page.

You may be keen to register a good domain name as soon as possible, and if you want to use a particular company or product name this is sensible enough. However, if you are just taking your first steps on the Web to see what you can do, it's probably better to use a free hosting service at first and wait to see how you get on before committing money to formal registration and web hosting.

REGISTERING A DOMAIN NAME

We're all familiar with memorable telephone numbers or abbreviated addresses used in adverts, and for just the same reasons you probably want to use a 'friendly' domain name for your website. To do this you will need to pay the relevant registration body and pay someone to hold your domain name registrations on their **domain name server** (usually whoever hosts your actual website).

Within certain limits you can choose your own domain name – the main limits being that no-one else has already registered the same name and that it fits into the recognized naming scheme. The name may contain no spaces or punctuation other than hyphens. Uppercase and lowercase letters are treated as identical in the domain name system.

The name scheme includes a suffix to indicate the origin or nature of the registered user. The most common endings are `.com` for US and international commercial users (almost two-thirds of all registered names), `.org` for non-profit, and `.net` for network related businesses. In the UK, `.co.uk` is used for commercial and `.org.uk` for non-profit organizations. There are many more suffixes, including complete sets for every country in the world, but those are the most commonly seen in the UK (apart from academic domains, `.edu` and `.ac.uk`, which are available only to accredited educational bodies).

At the start of 2000 there were around 11 million domain names registered worldwide, so the chances of your favoured name having been taken already are considerable! If not, you may want to jump in quickly with a registration to protect it at modest cost.

To select a suitable name, take a look at the search facilities on the naming authorities' websites. These are at www.nic.uk for names ending .uk, or at www.networksolutions.org for .com, .net and .org addresses.

To register one of these addresses for yourself, you need to use an intermediary company (a naming authority member). These advertise in the Internet magazines and online. You can find a full list of UK members at www.nic.uk/members. Registration companies can charge what they like for their services and yearly renewal (the actual cost is only a few pounds), but for the money you may get extra services such as website forwarding or free web space. US registrations cost $70 for two years, and most UK registration companies can also handle US registrations for you.

The easiest way to register a domain is usually to do it as part of a package deal from whoever is going to host your website, and often it will be 'thrown in for free', although of course you pay for it somewhere along the line. It is definitely worth shopping around on the Web for the best deals to suit you.

TOOLS OF THE TRADE

Web pages are not restricted to displaying plain text – even the simplest sites usually make use of different type styles and sizes, colour and control of page layout. Amazingly all this is achieved by sending simple text messages across the Internet to your browser.

The secret lies in using an agreed '**mark-up language**', with special codes inserted in the text to indicate changes of style, links to other pages, placement of pictures, and so on. As you will read later, there are advanced tools available that will shield you from the technicalities, but it will help you to appreciate the capabilities and limitations of these tools if you have a basic knowledge of what is going on 'under the hood'.

SIMPLE HTML

Each web page is stored as a simple text file that you can create with Windows *Notepad* or any word processor. As well as the text to be displayed, this file has the layout marked up using a coding scheme called **Hypertext Mark-up Language** (HTML). Unfortunately, owing to the break-neck pace of Web development, HTML is something of a moving target, with new features being added all the time. This makes it very difficult for advanced website authors and their software to keep in step with browser developments, but the basics of web page coding have changed little since the Web was first designed.

Tagging along

To separate mark-up codes from the text itself, all the codes are enclosed in angle brackets <like this>. Anything within these brackets will not be displayed as such and forms what is commonly called a **tag**, which will be interpreted by the browser to control the page design. Most commands include a start and end pair of mark-up codes. For example, to display

This word is *italic* and this word is **bold**

the web page would contain the following marked-up text:

```
This word is <I>italic</I> and
this word is <B>bold</B>
```

As you can see, for simple effects the end code is simply the start code prefixed with an oblique stroke /. You can use uppercase or lowercase in tags (for example <B> or <b>), but it is more common to stick to lowercase. It is also possible to mark-up the bold and italic effects using codes <STRONG> and <EM> (emphasis) instead of <B> and <I> respectively. This is in line with a web page philosophy of telling the browser the intention of the layout rather than the exact mechanical details. This allows the user to choose some alternative way of indicating strong text or emphasized text that suits them (maybe by means of colour, for example).

By default, the browser ignores ordinary line endings and any multiple spaces in the text you send to it, and regards it all as one long piece of text to be reformatted to suit the display width of the viewer's browser. Of course, you may want to force new lines and paragraphs at certain points, and there are simple codes for doing this. `<P>` is used at the start of a paragraph and `</P>` at the end in order to space it correctly. The code `<BR>` can also be used to cause a single line break. It is one of the few tags that do not need a matched ending tag – it simply causes a new line to be started wherever it appears in the text. There is also a `<PRE></PRE>` tag pair, which indicate that the enclosed text has been 'preformatted' and should be reproduced exactly as laid out in the HTML file. Other simple tag pairs include:

- `<CENTER>`your text`</CENTER>` to centre a paragraph horizontally (note the use of US spellings)
- `<H1>`…`<H6>`Heading text`</H1>`…`</H6>` to specify a standard heading level from 1 through to 6.

Headings also cause a new paragraph to be started

Again notice that the tags indicate that a given heading level is required, for example `<H2>`Heading at level 2`</H2>`, but do not actually specify what font size or style should be used for a heading of the chosen level. The browser is responsible for picking something appropriate and consistent, according to the users' preferences. There are more advanced codes that do specify absolute font sizes and styles, but pages that stick to the basic codes have the greatest chance of showing something sensible on the widest range of browsers.

There are dozens of tags providing facilities for more advanced layout elements such as bulleted lists, table layouts, option buttons, checkboxes and forms. To list all the tags available in HTML would take many pages, but comprehensive lists are available in books dedicated to HTML and in online tutorials (*see* **Going further with HTML**, *opposite*).

CONSTRUCTING A PAGE

Although browsers are very forgiving, and will display a simple line fragment such as the example above, a web page is more properly enclosed in a standard sequence of codes that give overall structure to the page:

`<HTML>`   indicates the start of a HTML document

`<HEAD>`   indicates that header information follows

`<TITLE>`   your page title goes here`</TITLE>`

`</HEAD>`   indicates the end of the header

`<BODY>`   main body of your page`</BODY>`

`</HTML>`   the end of the HTML document

Time to try it for yourself. Open Windows *Notepad* and enter this text into a fresh document, exactly as it appears here:

```
<HTML><HEAD>

<TITLE>My first web page</TITLE>

</HEAD><BODY>

<H1>Hello world!</H1>

This is my first web page.

</BODY></HTML>
```

Then save it as a file with a name ending .htm (such as mypage.htm) to any convenient place on your hard disk. You have just created your first web page!

GOING FURTHER WITH HTML

We have only shown the basics of learning to write your own HTML code in this chapter. There are plenty of resources available if you want to take it further, including many large and often expensive books dedicated to the topic. You can also find a number of excellent HTML tutorials for free on the Web itself. Some of the best ones offer a facility to download the whole tutorial (which may be many pages long) as a single document for offline study or reprinting.

A notably good guide, *The Beginner's Guide to HTML*, comes from NCSA, where the first graphical web browser, *Mosaic*, was developed. The guide is at www.ncsa.uiuc.edu/General/Internet/WWW/HTMLPrimer.html, and it is also available for download as a single compact Acrobat PDF file.

A number of service providers' sites include links to HTML tutorials and other helpful files on the Web. There is an extensive list on Demon Internet at www.helpdesk.demon.net/products/homepages/tutorials.html (you don't have to be a Demon subscriber to access this).

To see the results of all this hard work you need to load the page in your browser, so if your browser isn't already running, start it up now. There is no need to go online for this exercise, so if your browser is set to dial up automatically click **Cancel** before it has had a chance to finish dialling and then click the **Work Offline** button. In the browser, press CTRL+O (**File Open**), click the **Browse** button and locate your file in the usual way. Click **OK** a couple of times and your page will be loaded up in the browser. It should look something like this (*see right*). Don't worry if it isn't exactly the same – remember that the browser may be set to interpret text styles differently according to user preferences.

If your page looks very different, or is blank, then double-check it carefully in the text editor – you will almost certainly find that you have missed an angle bracket or ending tag, or made some other small typing error. Although browsers are fairly forgiving, they are easily fooled. For example, if you missed the ending </H1> from the heading line, your browser will happily carry on showing the whole page in Heading 1 style until it reaches the end of the file. Moreover, missing out part of a structure element, such as </HEAD>, can cause the whole page to disappear.

Even if you make a major mistake in the coding, no harm is done, and you can always re-open your page in the text editor and track down the error. On more complex pages this can be easier said than done. You will see later that there are more foolproof ways to construct pages, and there are systems available that will check and debug your HTML code for you. If you make any changes to your code, in order to see the effect you must save it again, and then press the **Refresh** button (or shortcut key F5) to load a fresh copy of the file on view in the browser.

A CRITICAL EYE ON YOUR CODE

The 'Bobby' HTML validation service at www.cast. org/bobby takes a thorough look through the coding of any web page you point it to, and then presents a very detailed report of any errors or poor coding practice that it spots. Don't be disheartened by the results – it is very picky, but also very instructive!

CHECK YOUR SOURCES

Before leaving the browser, right-click the page and choose **View Source** from the pop-up menu. This will re-open the current web page in a text editor (usually *Notepad*) where you can study the coding of the page and make alterations if you want. This is a really useful feature, particularly when looking at other people's web pages. If you are curious to see how a particular page has been built, or even to 'borrow' a little bit of coding from it, you can view its source to see exactly how it was done. Many of the fancier pages you will come across have horrendously obscure coding generated by authoring tools (*see later in this chapter*) or by expert programmers, but others will be based on the sort of simple, understandable HTML that we have been considering, and these can be very helpful.

AUTHORING TOOLS

Although constructing your own site in raw HTML can be very instructive and satisfying, it may not be the best use of your time if you want to create an appealing site quickly. To give yourself a head start in web page construction, you will be better off using one of the many **authoring tools** available. These are to websites what word processors are to writing a book – they provide an array of tools and views to help you construct a document looking just the way you want it without worrying too much about the technicalities.

As with all things to do with the Web, there is a huge range to choose from, ranging from free to very expensive and sophisticated. Many authoring tools are available in older or restricted versions on free disks or as downloads from the Web, so you can try before you buy. The only problem with this approach is that, once you have learnt to use a trial version competently, because of the effort you have put into learning it you may not want to give it up even if it doesn't suit you exactly. Which is, of course, exactly why the trial versions are given away so freely!

Web authoring tools come in several distinct flavours (and some interesting mixtures):

HTML editors simply provide a more efficient environment in which to edit the raw HTML code, assisting you to select tags, ensuring they are used properly, and checking the overall structure of the page. If you want to deal directly with the HTML code, then a HTML editor will save you time with the details and help you write error-free code more easily.

WYSIWYG editors take things a stage further, showing you the effect of your editing as it will appear in the browser. This is the easiest way for someone who has no interest at all in the technicalities needed to construct attractive pages. The simpler (cheaper) WYSIWYG editors are often quite limited in the range of effects they can handle accurately, but the more advanced ones will let you easily construct complex pages that would take days to code yourself. It's worth noting also that many modern office applications such as *Microsoft Office 2000* and *Corel WordPerfect Office 2000* can also generate sophisticated web pages directly from office documents.

Online editors are offered by many of the free website providers as a means of letting you set up a basic **home page**, or several pages, with no technical knowledge and no software tools other than your browser. Typically they require you to slot your own pictures and words into a template page that you have chosen from the range on offer. Despite their simplicity and the cost of being online while you use them, online editors can be an excellent way to get started with a 'web presence' while you consider the options for developing your pages further.

CHOOSE YOUR WEAPONS

Only you can decide which sort of tool will suit you best. If you simply want to get a page or two on the Web with the least fuss, then an **online editor** from one of the free web space providers will probably suit you best and will involve no extra purchases or software installation.

However, if you want to create a more varied and attractive site laid out to your own design, and you don't mind installing some substantial software, then you should find that a **WYSIWYG editor** lets you achieve nice results with the minimum of technical knowledge.

If you want to learn raw HTML coding or you are interested in the technicalities for their own sake, then a **HTML editor** will provide what you need and will be much quicker to use than a plain text editor.

Commercial packages often support more than one of these editing methods and provide other utilities for processing pictures or creating special HTML elements, such as pictures with clickable **hotspots**. In particular, the WYSIWYG editors usually include a HTML editor as an alternative way to view and deal with tricky bits of code. Most will allow you to import HTML code or complete pages that you have written in another package.

Advanced packages include various site management tools that let you visualize and organize the overall structure of multi-page websites and their resources (text, pictures, links and so on). These are a great help when it comes to adding in new pages, reviewing or reorganizing a site (see **Planning your website**, *page 47, and* **Building your site**, *page 72*).

The remainder of this chapter takes a closer look at a few typical packages available in the three categories. Bear in mind that newer versions and completely new products for the Web are appearing all the time. It's also worth checking cover disks from magazines for free copies of earlier versions of the latest web editors. These are often provided as tasters for the current version, with a special upgrade offer, but the earlier version may in fact be all you need.

HTML EDITORS

Many pure HTML editors nowadays are freeware or shareware, or come as part of an advanced WYSIWYG editor package. They are usually centred around a HTML text editing window with colour coding to distinguish text and code elements. Buttons are provided for quick insertion of HTML tags, and some form of clipboard may be provided for temporary handling of code fragments.

Webedit from San Diego Software is a typical raw HTML editor for those who don't want to be shielded from the works! It has drop-down toolbar items and colour-coded text windows, and will check HTML code for validity. (Standard edition about $80, Pro version about $130, both downloadable. More details from www.sandiego.com/webedit.)

HotDog Express Professional is a comprehensive tool with powerful features, including some site management and built-in FTP uploading to your web server. Although popular, earlier versions were criticized for sluggish performance. Version 5.5 has been considerably enhanced to speed things up and has won many awards.(Downloadable for about $130, more details from www.sausage.com.) There is also a Junior version for children to produce websites in four simple stages based on templates.

Jesse6 (*below*) is a fully-featured freeware HTML editor with **JavaScript** and **Java applet** support, enhancements for *Internet Explorer*, multiple clipboards, full HTML documentation and instructions for beginners and die-hards alike. You can test your web pages in the browser of your choice, so you can see exactly what the page will look like on the Web. Controls are provided to add lists, bullets, numbers, tables, hover-over buttons, links, fonts, and more.

Jesse6 has a scratchpad for holding fragments of code that you may want to re-use, and a built in image viewer supporting BMP, GIF and JPEG graphics file formats, so you can browse through images and insert them into your documents automatically. (2.4Mb, downloadable free from `newwave.net/~yogi/jesse6.html`.)

At the more polished end of the scale, **Allaire Homesite** is a powerful HTML editor available in its own right or as part of some WYSIWYG packages. It is centred around raw text editing, but has comprehensive buttons and resource windows showing thumbnail images of pictures and other resources that may be dragged into place in the HTML code. A 'snippets palette' performs much the same function as the scratchpad in *Jesse6*. There is a **JavaScript** wizard to allow non-programmers to insert some of the fancier effects such as dynamic transitions (colour changes, wipes, and so on). *Homesite* also has excellent support for the construction of tables and forms, and a code-checking utility, *Codesweeper*, which can tidy up your work automatically. (Version 4 is about £80; more details from `www.allaire.com`.)

WYSIWYG EDITORS

Comprehensive WYSIWYG editors are more substantial pieces of software that usually include additional site and resource management tools and some form of HTML editor. Some excellent programs, for example *Dreamweaver* and *NetObjects Fusion*, are quite expensive for simple home use, but there are also some very competent cheap, or even free, WYSIWYG editors.

Microsoft FrontPage Express is the page-editing component of Microsoft's comprehensive *FrontPage* web publishing program and is supplied free with *Internet Explorer*. *FrontPage Express* gives you the same powerful facilities for editing and formatting web pages that come in the full package. Microsoft's *Web Publishing Wizard*, a simple utility for uploading files easily to your ISP, is also supplied free. If you later upgrade to *FrontPage 2000* (part of the Microsoft *Office 2000* suite), you get the rest of the *FrontPage* software, including powerful site management software. The sample site shown later in this book was developed using *Front Page Express*, so you can obtain all the software you need to follow the examples in the book on widely available, free CD-ROMs. (As well as the free CD-ROMs the package is downloadable; more details from www.microsoft.co.uk.)

Netscape Composer is a straightforward WYSIWYG editor, which is supplied free with the full *Netscape Communicator* suite 4.0 or later. The suite can be downloaded free from Netscape's website, or you can order it on a CD-ROM for a handling charge. It is also possible to get it by requesting a free sign-up CD-ROM from NetscapeOnline. The software provides a clean editing environment with a composition button bar that has buttons to insert the usual web page elements such as links, images and tables, and a good spellchecker. A formatting bar includes easy drop-down selectors for standard heading tags, typefaces, colours and sizes. The built-in HTML editor is implemented as a **Java applet**.

It is rather slow to start up, and offers no colour coding or other aids, but it does permit basic editing of the source HTML code. (On CD-ROM or downloadable free from www.netscapeonline.co.uk/help/orderform.htm or 0800 923 0009; more details at www.netscape.com.)

Adobe PageMill 3 is the latest version of a long-standing package in widespread use. It offers good raw HTML editing as well as fast WYSIWYG working, and is particularly good at transforming Microsoft *Office* word processor documents and spreadsheets into web pages (this ability is also built into the latest versions of Microsoft *Word* and *Excel*). *PageMill* provides an integrated HTML editor, and you can switch quickly between source-code view and regular WYSIWYG preview modes. It also has good facilities for creating **frames** interactively by dragging frame dividers across the page with the mouse. Elements may be dragged off one page and onto another via a 'pageboard' for quick cloning of images and effects, and there are good facilities for rapidly creating forms with the mouse. The package also includes *PhotoShop LE* for high-quality image preparation, and a large collection of web-ready images, sounds, video clips, animations, Java applets, and customizable templates. (About £90, downloadable as a 13Mb trial version; more details from www.adobe.co.uk.)

SoftQuad HoTMetaL PRO 6 is the latest in a venerable line of web page editors and has been popular with home users and professionals alike. It is a comprehensive package that offers optional preset layouts and structures, drag-and-drop animation and graphics effects, spellchecker, site management utilities and automated file uploading to your web server. The full workspace includes an outrageous number of toolbars and buttons, but these can be customized or hidden. A distinctive feature – also offered by *FrontPage 2000* – is **tags on view** editing, which is a cross between WYSIWYG and raw HTML editing, showing an essentially visual layout with small symbols inserted to represent formatting tags. *HoTMetaL PRO*'s table editing is not as slick as some other programs, but its facilities for form building are very good. (About £110; more details from www.softquad.co.uk.)

Tags on view in HoTMetaL Pro

ONLINE EDITORS

Online editors are aimed at users who want to create a very simple website – perhaps just one page – with the absolute minimum of complication, and are most often provided with free web space supported by advertising. They are based on template layouts provided by the server and customized by options, pictures and words given online by the user. Although this way of working puts clear limits on the range of effects and page complexity possible, nonetheless they are an easy way for inexperienced users to produce smart pages. Ironically, although the pages may be simple, preplanning your pages offline pays off significantly by minimizing your online time.

Yahoo!'s **Geocities** is a popular online system of free web pages organized into themed 'communities' named after countries and cities of the world. This is a rather quirky arrangement, but some users have built excellent information resources within *Geocities* and their pages regularly turn up in search engine results. As well as the *Yahoo! PageBuilder* to construct a good-looking page, *Geocities* offers free clipart, headlines and guest books to enhance your site. An uncommon feature for a free website, supplied by *Geocities*, is **streaming media**, a system for offering audio and video clips on your pages (*see* **Putting on the style**, *page 136*). *Geocities* offers users 15Mb of disk space, and the system is paid for by a small pop-up advert. (More details from www.geocities.com.)

Tripod offers several ways to build your web pages within its own *Homepage Builder* system, or you can work with other software packages (even a text editor) and upload it (the only independent page-building software specifically not supported is Microsoft

FrontPage!). Tripod's simplest option, the *QuickPage* builder, can help you create a page in a very short time with no knowledge of HTML. The *Custom Editor* allows you to create or edit a page directly in HTML. Tripod members' pages are categorized rather like *Geocities*', but using rather broad categories of common-interest 'pods' (looked after by 'poderators'!). Members are entitled to 12MB of disk space, and the system is paid for by small advertising pop-ups. (More details at www.tripod.com.)

ZyWeb page builder is another online web authoring system that enables users with no graphical or technical expertise to produce smart web pages with custom graphics in just a few minutes. *ZyWeb* gives you 10MB of web space for your files, pictures and web pages, including a proper work area of your own where you can upload, store and organize your materials prior to placing them on pages. Registering online takes only a minute, then you simply choose the type of web page you want to create from the professionally designed range and, using the online editor, customize the pages. You can alter the text, change the graphics and links, and even edit the page layout, choosing a new theme that will be consistently applied to the whole page. To pay for the service a small banner advert will appear at the bottom of your pages, and *ZyWeb* may remove any pages that have not been edited or accessed for over 60 days. (More details from www.zyworld.com.)

PLANNING YOUR WEBSITE

The single most important thing to keep in mind about your website is what you want it to achieve – what is its objective? Everything else flows from that. Setting out without a clear objective would be like heading off down the motorway with no idea of where you are trying to go: you could take a lot of time to end up in quite the wrong place, or even back where you started!

A website is a communication medium and, just like a book, a radio programme, or a lecture, its purpose is to affect the knowledge or behaviour of its audience. So it's also very important that you think about who is in your audience and how they will use your website.

WHAT ARE YOUR OBJECTIVES?

If you are constructing a website for your own use, then only you can really decide what its objectives are. If your objectives have been set by others, you will still need to make sure they are framed in a useful way before you start out. You may find this the hardest part of planning your own website and you could be tempted to skip it, but try not to. It will pay off.

You might simply want to create a site for your own interest and satisfaction, which is great. But even if your main objective is just to learn about website construction and have fun along the way, it's best to have secondary objectives for your practice pages so you can judge for yourself how well you have done and what you could do better.

If you are going to create a site with several pages, the chances are that you will have an overall aim for the site: for example, 'After visiting this site, visitors will want to come to my town.' You will also have secondary aims for individual pages: for example, 'After reading this page visitors will know exactly where my town is,' or, 'After reading this page visitors will know what restaurants are in my town.'

Of course, life is never as simple as that, and you shouldn't let formal objectives be a barrier to having fun along the way. For a site that really works, clear objectives are the strong, underlying fibres to the attractive fabric that visitors see.

KNOW YOUR AUDIENCE

A key part of achieving your objectives is to know who your audience is, or at least what parts of your audience you are most interested in. The chances are that you may have different objectives for different sectors of your audience, and you will need to categorize them so that you can adapt your approach to each.

Don't try to think of every last individual type of visitor, just broad groupings (preferably no more than three), or you will find it difficult to keep your style focused. How you categorize your visitors will depend on the subject area of your site. For example, for an entertainment site

BEING OBJECTIVE

This isn't a book about setting objectives, but here are a few tips that will point you in the right direction.

Keep it simple You should be able to express your main objective in one simple sentence, probably phrased in terms of what change you will have brought about in your visitors. For example, 'Visitors will have learned what a great place my village is to live in,' or, 'Visitors will want to buy my watercolour paintings.'

Be realistic If you are starting out in web design, don't set yourself an impossibly high target. That will only lead to frustration and dissatisfaction. Don't expect your website to change the world overnight; just think about what you can impart to each ordinary visitor. And don't try to do everything at once – remember that every journey starts with the first step.

Make it testable This means making sure you can test how well your site achieves what you intended. Technical testing is easy, but what really counts is whether your pages satisfy their objectives. This may seem a bit over the top for simple hobby work, but if you baked a cake or brewed your own beer you would want to know how it tasted, wouldn't you?

you might divide your visitors by age (say, kiddies, teenagers and adults), and on a local area information site you might divide them into residents, business people and tourists.

Ideally it should become second nature to put yourself in your visitor's place, cast a critical eye over what you have done and assess how well it is likely to achieve your objective. Of course, it's even better if you can get some 'guinea pigs' to take a look at your site and tell you what they think. It's also very instructive to watch someone else navigating around your pages for the first time – they may have difficulties or fresh ideas that never occurred to you when you designed the site.

Once your site is 'live' on the Web, there are more techniques you can use to get to know your audience better and to devise ways to improve your site to meet their needs (see **Visitor feedback**, page 54), or to work at getting more of your intended audience to your site (see **Pulling the crowds**, page 166). Of course, the great thing about a website is that, unlike a book, even after it is published and in the hands of its readers, you can revise it easily and cheaply. This means that, if you find people aren't using it the way you expected, or are clearly having difficulty finding something important, you can change the words or layout to help them. You might even alter your whole approach to the subject, or add a completely new section. And, of course, you can also fix minor errors and keep the site generally up to date and relevant (see **Maintaining your site**, page 178).

INTERACTION

One way or another, the objectives of almost all websites are to teach visitors something or to persuade them to do something. It might be something simple, such as to tell them that there is a regular bus service to your village, or to persuade them to travel on the bus instead of driving. Just as in conventional teaching, one of the most powerful ways to do this effectively on the Web is to employ interaction.

If your visitors become actively involved in discovering information from your site, that information is much more likely to stick. And if you can make it a fun experience, visitors are more likely to stay around longer and to come back for more. In fact, this is a key factor in the whole success of the Web. Web surfing is not a purely passive affair, even when it is done by someone sitting alone at a computer screen. The visitor has continuous control and frequent choices to make on where to go next, what to look at and what to skip over. This makes web browsing a more enjoyable experience and improves the chances that people spending time on your site will be receptive to your message.

So the Web itself is interactive at a basic level of navigating from site to site. All websites with linked pages have a level of interaction within themselves, and even if you only provide simple page navigation, you are on the right road. There are many other ways to engage your visitors, however, and some are very simple to set up and administer.

For example, you can offer visitors the chance to zoom in on a picture – to see more detail or another angle – by making the illustration itself a link to another picture. This is also a valuable technique for

Clicking a small 'thumbnail' picture on this web page opens a larger version of the picture

minimizing page loading times while making detail available for those who are willing to wait.

A powerful extension of this interaction is to provide a simple **virtual reality** picture that visitors can fully control, scrolling it left and right, tilting it up and down, or even rolling it through 360°. Simple tools are available for generating this sort of thing, and are especially useful if you have a digital camera or scanner (*see* **Putting on the style**, *page 136*).

Another simple type of interaction is with web forms. If you have ordered or registered for anything on the Web, you will almost certainly have seen a web form before. These can be as simple as a single text box to be filled in, or extremely complex. Coding the forms directly in HTML can be a bit fiddly, but most authoring tools provide good support for easy interactive 'drawing' of

A typical web form with checkboxes and a drop-down selector

forms on your web pages.

Visitors who have taken the trouble to fill in your form will feel they have invested something in their visit to your site, and that it has given them a more substantial service. Of course, their expectations will also have been raised, and you should make sure that they receive whatever benefit you promised in return for completing your form.

ADVANCED INTERACTION

Advanced types of interaction are possible using various computer programming languages and automation systems. These allow web pages to deliver complex, fast and flexible responses to users' actions, more like traditional computer software applications. These programs may be server-based or browser-based, depending on whether the programmed instructions are carried out on the server before sending the page to the browser, or whether the instructions are transferred to the browser as **applets** in a web page and then executed on the viewer's own computer.

Although creating such software from scratch may be beyond you in the early stages of learning how to create your own website, many authoring tools include a collection of ready-to-use browser-based applets to include in your own pages. Many web hosts offer ready-made server-based scripts for common tasks such as providing guest books (*see* **Visitor feedback**, *below*).

VISITOR FEEDBACK

Visitors who come to your site by anything other than sheer chance will have their own objectives and their own expectations of what your site will do for them. They may not have sat down and thought about these things, but they will have them all the same. Ideally you should try to meet or exceed your visitors' expectations, while still achieving your own objectives. Of course, to do this you also need to have some idea of what those expectations were.

In a perfect (but boring) world, your objectives and the visitors' would be the same. Unless your site has a very simple factual information content this is not likely to occur. But if your site has a useful or interesting story to tell, and does it well, your visitors may well forget all about their initial objectives and enjoy pursuing yours instead! Just think about your own web browsing experiences – how often have you ended up reading or doing something completely different from what you set out to do, but found it enjoyable and interesting all the same?

The most powerful tool to help you fine-tune these things is feedback from your audience. Again, this is much more easily arranged with a website than with other publishing methods, and your visitors will appreciate the chance to tell you how they feel about the site just as much as you should value hearing from them.

The simplest sort of feedback is people voting with their feet! You can easily arrange to keep a simple check on the number of people visiting any of your pages, and review the numbers as you make changes or promote your site. This might seem a very mechanical technique that doesn't involve the visitor actively, but many sites make a feature of an on-page **visitor counter** that is visual fun for visitors as well as being informative. There are several places on the Web that specialize in providing counters for use by other sites (*see* **Pulling the crowds**, *page 166, and* **Maintaining your site**, *page 178*).

A novel counter generated by Java

A more substantial feedback tool that also provides something in return for the visitor is the guest book (*see panel on next page*).

GUEST BOOKS

As the name suggests, these are the online equivalent of the sort of book you might find in a guest house or local museum, where visitors can leave their names and addresses along with a short comment about their visit. Not only will you receive direct feedback of visitors' opinions, but you can also ask for a few personal details such as their age group and home country or town. This provides an opportunity to do a little informal research on your visitors.

The main payback for your visitors should be that you modify the site in the light of their comments, and hopefully improve the experience for them! However, that's a rather long-term process, and most sites provide a more immediate spin-off from the guest book by allowing visitors to browse the details of previous visitors for their own interest.

Most of the free online authoring websites offer a guest book as a standard option.

These are particularly popular on personal and hobby sites as they cost nothing and are self-maintaining. They can also be informative and fun.

You could take the view that, if your site is working perfectly, visitors would come along, do everything you intended them to do, learn everything you intended them to learn, and leave – never to be seen again. But you will want to develop your site, and really it would be better if visitors come back again from time to time to get the most out of it. It's best to give some thought to this from the outset and, as you are planning each part

A typical guest book

of your site, consider what you can do to encourage your visitors to come back frequently (*see* **Pulling the crowds**, *page 166*).

LOOK AND FEEL

All websites have a 'look and feel'. Sometimes the look is very evident and easily described (for example, simple text in a formal layout on a plain background), and sometimes it is more difficult to describe concisely (for example 'arty', 'bright', 'gimmicky'). The feel of a site is influenced by its writing style, the navigation methods and interaction employed.

When you are considering how to approach different types of visitor, you may well want to adopt a completely different look and feel for, say, children and adults, even if the content and objectives are much the same for both. On the other hand, on a site where you are categorizing visitors differently, for example on a business site, you may well keep the same look and feel for all, but vary the objectives and content substantially.

For your first forays into website creation it's best to stick to simple styles of presentation. The simpler the style, the easier it is to get it right. The most common problems to afflict beginners come from trying to cram too much on one page, and using too many varieties of colour, typeface and alignment. Unless you specifically want to use outrageous design and visual shock value, develop a consistent, uncluttered style for text and layout.

Collins GEM This isn't to say that your site has to be boring or unattractive. As you browse around the Web, keep a look out for those simple little extras that are used to liven up web pages without overburdening the design or distracting the user too far from the main message. These are known in the trade as '**eye candy**' and, like sweets, they are best taken in moderation! Often you will see things you can adapt to your own purposes or which spur you to an idea of your own. Of course, you shouldn't lift something wholesale from another site unless it is offered for that purpose, but basing a feature of your own on someone else's idea is part and parcel of site design.

In look and feel, magazines are perhaps the closest traditional publishing medium to a website. They have sections of pure prose with occasional visual splashes, and other pages featuring more jazzy graphics. Readers are expected to jump around from item to item, to skip items of less interest, and perhaps to cut out and keep items of great interest. So take a look at some of the techniques that magazines use, but remember that a printed page can carry far more detail than a computer screen can. Web pages have their limits!

Typography and page design are major subjects in their own right, but if you keep things simple and consistent, and listen to what your visitors say (*see* **Visitor feedback**, *page 54*), you shouldn't go far wrong. You can find out a lot more about the art of page design later in this book (*see* **Putting on the style**, *page 136*).

STRUCTURAL DESIGN

You may want just a single page on your site, and that's fine if you can create a clear single-page layout of what you want to say (for example, for a simple personal profile page). However, most subjects call for at least a few pages to make a worthwhile site, and some simple site navigation work can actually increase a visitor's involvement and commitment, even if the content could all have fitted a single page!

The easiest approach is to look at what you need to get your message across (remember your objectives!) and, if you can't fit it comfortably on one screen, work out how to break it up logically and clearly into a set of linked pages. At first, concern yourself only with how the pages and their links will appear to visitors, not with what happens behind the scenes – that comes later.

Navigation

If your site calls for only a few pages on separate topics, or for separate aspects of one topic, then it will probably be appropriate to have a single introductory page (the **home page**), with individual links straight to each of the other pages in the site. At the very least, each of those pages should have a clear link back to the home page, so that visitors can always return to a known starting point. These links are often indicated by some little icon, such as a house, or a logo applicable to the whole site.

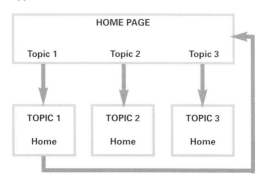

Depending on how the topics are related, it may also be appropriate for the various pages to have links to each other, so visitors can go from topic to topic without returning to the home page. Or the pages may be

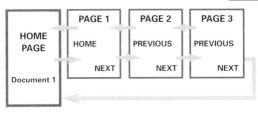

arranged in a sort of logical ring, so that each page has a link to the page that comes before it and after it in sequence, and the last page links back to the first.

Drawing simple flow diagrams similar to those shown here will help you visualize and plan your site navigation routes. Site management tools often have features to show your site in this way, but they don't always display things very clearly.

If you have to present a long piece of text, and would prefer not to have too much vertical scrolling of the page, you can split it into several pages. A common rule of thumb is not to present a page that is more than two

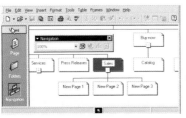

Site navigation in FrontPage 2000

to three screens long, so that readers don't have to wait so long for each page to load and won't lose track of where they are in the document.

When you split a single document over several pages, you need to make a link from your introduction to the first page in the set and at least link the pages in a forwards direction, with a link back home from the final page in the sequence. For the reader's convenience, more links are usually provided, with links back to the 'top' of the document and the home page from every page, and perhaps a link back to the previous page for quicker re-reading.

If you don't mind encouraging visitors to print out your document for reading offline, you should also consider offering a 'printable' version. This is usually just a web page on which the entire document appears as one long, scrolling item. The visitor's browser will take care of splitting it into pages as it prints.

Where offline use or reprinting of a document is important, you can also make it available as a downloadable file simply by placing the file on your web server and providing a link to it (*see* **Building your site**, *page 72*). More advanced options for providing print-formatted documents are available using *Adobe Acrobat* **PDF** (*see* **Putting on the style**, *page 136*).

FRAMES

To present more complex site navigation schemes you can use **frames**. These offer a way to divide up larger sites, whilst still allowing visitors to navigate easily and understand where they are. The browser window is divided into several smaller frames, with or without visible dividers, and when visitors click links in a 'navigation frame' the result is to change the content of a 'content frame'. The choices remain visible in the navigation frame, often with the current choice highlighted.

A typical example, shown below, has major divisions of the site offered in a frame across the top (Products, Support, Contacts, What's new, and so on), and topic areas within the selected major area are offered in a frame down the side (Feature list, Free trial, Ordering, and so on). When a new major section is selected in the top frame, the list of options down the left side changes to reflect the topics within that area.

Frames can be quite awkward to code, and the site structure can become complex, so they are best handled

Frame-controlled navigation across the top and down the side of a product site

with an authoring tool that has suitable management facilities for them. Frames are inaccessible to some of the older browsers still in use, to special-needs browsers and also to some of the modern hand-held gizmos such as mobile phones with built-in browsers. If such visitors are important to you, provide alternative, non-framed pages.

OTHER NAVIGATION TECHNIQUES

There are many other ways to navigate a website. Variety is good, but you need to make sure that the navigation options are clear to your visitors. It doesn't matter how clever or dazzling your site navigation is, it is no use at all if visitors can't very quickly work out how to use it.

A long-standing technique that is unique to the Web is the clickable image, or **image map**, in which visitors can jump to various pages according to which part of a

graphic image they click. The obvious use for this is in making spatial choices, such as clicking places on a map to go to information about those places, or clicking parts of a

Clicking this image provides information about the different parts of a tropical tank

machine to learn more about those parts. Most authoring packages have special tools to help you define clickable regions on images and set up the links to the required pages.

Drop-down selectors are a useful alternative way of offering multiple navigation choices. They are particularly suitable when you have a long list of options to fit in and don't want to resort to complex layouts. The drop-down also makes a very useful adjunct to a clickable image for more precise selection or for visitors who may be unfamiliar with the parts in the image. For example, a list of countries or regions could be used alongside a clickable map for those unfamiliar with the geography, or to allow finer selection of particular towns within regions.

Site maps, as the name suggests, are intended to help visitors orient themselves in the structure of your site. They can be as simple as a contents list or as complex as a flow diagram showing how the whole site is linked, with the visitor's current location highlighted. Some of the most sophisticated site maps are used as both orientation and navigation tools. The advanced example shown here uses a Java applet to generate an attractive list of site headings, with

Advanced site navigation on the UK Ordnance Survey site

expandable drop-down sections to show the detail within each area. There are three levels of subdivision, and any of the items may be clicked to jump straight in at the level required.

In your web wanderings you will come across many variations on the above ideas, and several more advanced possibilities. The page shown below from www.vacationvillas.net makes a good job of the difficult goal of maintaining a simple, clear design while deploying several navigation and presentation techniques to good effect in a single page.

As always, keep your eyes open for good ideas, bookmark sites of interest, and perhaps use the **View Source** function to take a peek at how these have been achieved. *See also* **Building your site**, *page 72*.

FILE TYPES

Your website might include all sorts of files, such as sound, film clips, office documents or software. Some of these will be sent out in response to automatic requests from the browser (for example, as background music to a page), and others will be sent only on user demand (for example, a request to download a software file). The file types are distinguished in just the same way as they are on a PC, by means of a file name extension – a full stop followed by a few letters after the file name.

Basic web pages have the standard extension `.htm` or `.html`, depending on the particular authoring tool and server. On sites designed for, or by, PC users, other files tend to use the same extensions that they would on a PC. For example, a Microsoft *Word* document would end `.doc` and an executable piece of software would end `.exe`.

The server is generally blind to these file types and simply sends whatever file is requested, but the browser's decisions as to what to do with the files it receives are based on the file extensions. For example, if a `.doc` file is retrieved from the server, the browser will usually ask you whether you want to open it immediately in *Word* or to save it to disk for later use.

PLANNING YOUR SERVER STRUCTURE

In computer terms, your website is just a collection of files stored on a web server. The server receives requests from browsers around the world and sends out the requested files. In most cases the server knows nothing of the logical layout of your site, and the way your site is structured for navigation is not necessarily mirrored in the way the files are structured on your web host. The server doesn't even know, for example, what pictures are included in a particular page.

When a browser requests a new page, the server sends just the text file corresponding to that page. If the browser then sees that there are various pictures specified in the page, it issues separate requests to the server for those pictures and places them in the page when they arrive. From your own browsing you will be familiar with the situation that picture files are generally larger and slower to transfer than the main text of a web page. They continue to be filled in to spaces on the page for some time after the main text has arrived.

KEEPING YOUR SERVER TIDY

It is up to you (or your authoring tool) how the collection of files that makes up your site should be organized on the server. By default, your web hosting area will start out with a main directory and perhaps some standard subdirectories for specific purposes. You can create additional subdirectories for the organization of your files in much the same way as you organize files on your own computer's hard disk drive. You don't have to do this if you don't want to, or if you find it hard to handle filing system names, but if there are more than a few dozen files on your website it is probably a good idea to sort them out.

The main reason for subdividing the server files is to ease housekeeping activities such as backing up, updating files, and keeping a track of what is on the server. It is also necessary if you want to use different files of the same name (just as with the PC, no two files in a directory may have the same name). You can set up some useful tricks, such as switching between sets of pages in alternative languages without completely rewriting all the links. This is done by duplicating sections of the site structure in different directories (for example, `/mysite/english` and `/mysite/gaelic`) and editing just the text of the duplicate pages for the required language.

Many sites simply put pictures into a subdirectory – such as `/images` – and some authoring tools encourage this way of working, but it has little real advantage. More highly structured arrangements usually involve some degree of modelling the site's navigational organization. For example, if you have a site with three very distinct areas for prices, specifications and applications, plus a home page and a contacts page, you might have your files organized something like this:

`/`	home page and contacts page
`/prices`	product price pages
`/specs`	product specification pages

DIFFERENT STROKES...

Web directory names are separated by a forward slash /, rather than the PC's backslash \, but the purpose is the same. So www.mysite.co.uk/pictures/button1.gif refers to the GIF file button 1 in the subdirectory 'pictures' of your web server storage.

When your browser retrieves files from your local disk drive, for example during site development, you can usually use whichever suits you. However, when you enter separators in HTML code for your web pages, you should always use the forward slash /. If you are using an authoring tool it will probably take care of this detail for you.

Unlike on PCs, upper- and lowercase letters are often treated as significant in web server filenames. So MyFile.htm and myfile.htm might well refer to different files, even though a PC would treat them as identical. For safety, most web designers adopt a convention of always using lowercase file names.

Just as with your local drive, the top-level directory is usually referred to as the root folder. This is the place that a browser will request files from if someone comes to the main URL of your site (for example, www.mysite.co.uk). If someone enters just the basic URL of your website, with no specific page name, the web server will usually send back a default page such as index.htm or welcome.htm.

/apps	product application pages
/apps/pics	product application pictures

In the early days, while you have just a handful of files on the server, it is probably simplest to keep everything in the root directory. As things become more complex, a little advance planning of your site's storage and how you expect it to develop will really pay off in the long run. If you study the changing URLs as you navigate around some of the larger sites on the Web, you will soon start to see patterns in the way most web designers organize things.

If you are using an online website construction tool, you may have no choice about how to store your files. If you are developing your site with a text editor or HTML editor, then you are in full control of file locations, but any major rearrangement of files is likely to involve a lot of hard work updating all the links between various pages to reflect the changed locations. If you are using a more advanced authoring tool, it probably has site management facilities that will update all your links automatically if you ask it to move files around. These aren't always foolproof, so don't do it just for fun!

BUILDING YOUR SITE

This section covers the real work of creating your website. From your own wanderings on the Internet you probably already have some idea of the look and feel you want for the site, including how it is to be structured and navigated. You should also have a good idea of what you want your site to achieve and who your target audience is.

The real aim of this book is to show you how to build your own sites with ease and enjoyment, but it will make things much easier if we pick a sample topic and pretend that we are going to build the site 'for real'. We will generate a simple site with a fairly uniform page layout, and along the way we'll build in many of the features you have read about earlier, as well as a few new ones.

The subject of the sample site isn't really important – it could be your family, a hobby, sports activities, your business… anything. As our example, we'll build a site for people interested in a local area. In order to keep this first adventure into website design manageable, we will choose a small place (Gairloch, in Wester Ross, Scotland), and create representative pages to illustrate ideas that you can use as the basis for your own web pages later. We will start by creating a few simple pages with a minimum of fancy features, and then refine and extend these to create a more useful and attractive site.

As we progress, you will see **Try it now** sections that show you how to follow the development on your own PC using Microsoft *FrontPage Express*. The first of these sections explains in more detail how you can do this without staying online to the Internet. If you want to use a different authoring package, such as *Netscape Composer*, you should be able to follow quite easily using the equivalent commands and functions in your chosen package. The sample pages use the Verdana font, supplied with *Internet Explorer*. You can use another font, such as Arial, if you don't have Verdana installed on your system, but your pages won't look quite the same as in the examples shown. Alternatively, you can download Verdana free from Microsoft's website (*see* **Putting on the style**, *page 136*) for use with any other authoring tool.

If you don't want to construct the samples as you go along, you could also simply examine the sample pages on the Web and use the **View Source** command in your browser to look in detail at how they were built. The first **Try it now** section simply helps you get organized to follow the later sections.

OBJECTIVES AND AUDIENCE

The overall objective of the site will be to inform its web visitors about the local district in order to encourage tourists to visit this relatively isolated area. So the primary audience is potential tourists, and the site's content should be aimed at making them want to come to the area.

TRY IT NOW: GETTING READY

If you want to follow the **Try it now** sections exactly, the first thing to do is check that you have Microsoft *Internet Explorer* (version 4 or 5) and *FrontPage Express*, which is supplied along with *Internet Explorer* but is not always installed (*see* **Before you begin**, page 14).

If *FrontPage Express* is installed, it should appear on the **Programs** menu in the *Internet Explorer* folder, but occasionally it fails to show. Another way to check that it is installed is to start

FrontPage Express *on the Programs menu*

Internet Explorer, load a page, and take a look at the **File** menu – there should be an **Edit with FrontPage Express Editor** command available.

Edit with FrontPage Express *command in* Internet Explorer

If you have *Internet Explorer* installed, but not *FrontPage Express*, then you should re-run the *Internet Explorer* set-up program, following the instructions for a 'full installation', or a 'custom installation' with *FrontPage Express* and *Web Publishing Wizard* included in the selected components.

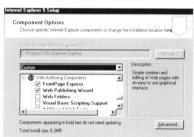

FrontPage Express *set-up*

So that you can work offline, with no telephone costs, you may prefer to download all the sample files used in the book, and install them on your own hard disk. To do this, use your browser to go to www.gairloch.co.uk/collins-gem, and follow the instructions and tips there.

If you don't want to carry out the **Try it now** exercises for yourself, but would simply like to look at the sample pages online, you can also browse them directly, starting from the same address.

Of course, it would be good for the site to encourage repeat visits from past tourists as well, and to provide information that would also be of use to local residents. In some parts of the site we might also want to distinguish overseas and UK readers, so that UK travellers don't have to wade through the extra information provided for international visitors. These are secondary audiences and objectives, and all your visitors' needs will overlap substantially, so it should be possible to design most pages to be of interest to all.

Developing the content

Your page designs must take into account the nature and amount of the information you want to present. In particular, you need to create layouts that can accommodate the right mix of text, images and navigation controls. So it will help a lot if you jot down the likely topics before you start creating the pages.

The topics featured in our sample site will include geographical information, travel information, tourist attractions, some local history, accommodation and links to other websites promoting the region, such as the tourist board. In practice, the greater part of the work required to create such a site is usually gathering the information and keeping it up to date, rather than building the site – unless you are building it for someone else who is providing all the words and images.

GATHERING THE MATERIALS

Sources of information and images for your site will depend very much on the subject, and may well include information from other websites. In the case of a local tourism site, likely sources of information include travel guides and brochures, tourist agencies, local history books and, of course, local knowledge. The core of your task is to bring together these sources of information and **transform** them into a suitable size and style for web presentation to your target audience. The process is much the same as preparing an essay or writing a book.

If you are developing a site about something of personal interest, then the chances are that you already know a lot about the subject. You will probably have a lot of useful sources of information and maybe people who can help you. Remember that you shouldn't lift content directly from someone else's work without permission. If you find pages of relevant and well-presented information on other websites, there may be no need to incorporate the material in your own site at all – you could just use the power of the Web to include **links** to those other sites (*see* **External links**, *page 112*). This avoids difficult questions of copyright (*see* **Copyright**, *opposite*).

WRITING THE WORDS

You may want to do this entirely for yourself, or you might get help from others. In any event, you would do well to enlist at least one other person to read through your material to check that it makes sense to others before parading it in front of the world! Apart from getting the facts right, the most important thing is to make sure that your style of writing is 'accessible' to your intended audience. As well as containing all the necessary information, it should be written in a style that your readers will find interesting and comfortable to read, otherwise you won't get your message across.

You should write simply and clearly, but in a way that keeps your visitors' interest. Readers' attention spans on web pages can be as short as two or three seconds – it is so easy to move away by clicking something that looks

COPYRIGHT

The following is not formal legal advice, just general guidance on the issue of copyright as it affects web publishers.

Copyright is the legal right to control the reproduction of any images, performances or text, usually until 70 years after the death of the author. The copyright may belong to the original creator of the piece, for example a photographer, or it may have been sold, for example to an agency. Owning a copyright-protected item does not necessarily mean having the right to reproduce it.

When you publish other people's work on your website, you must be sure that you have the copyright holder's permission or you could get into serious legal trouble. The fact that others may have already published it on their websites does not mean that you have permission to publish it on yours. Similarly, buying a picture, such as a postcard or an art print, does not give you the right to reproduce it.

Clipart and photo libraries are sold specifically for your own use, in which you pay for a licence to use the images as part of the product price, and it is best to stick to these sources if you need pictures that you cannot create or commission for yourself.

If you need to show material that is on another web page, the safest thing to do is simply create a link to that page and credit the source fully.

more interesting. It is easy enough to improve your wording later, but who knows how many people might decide not to come back if they came across something hard to read on your site? So try to get it reasonably right from the outset, even if that means leaving some things out until you are more practised.

Try to keep your style and presentation consistent across your site. This will make it easier for readers to understand the way you present things, and to appreciate the significance of different parts of the layout. If you have ever been involved with producing magazines or newsletters, you will be familiar with these issues already. Of course, you may not want your pages to be too predictable, or the site could become boring. This is a balance of judgement that you will have to take in the light of your intended audience, their expectations and your objectives.

A quick look through newspapers and newsletters could be very instructive. Look at the ones you find the most interesting and enjoyable to read, and see what style tips you can pick up. In particular, look at the way that articles are structured. Stories typically have a very brief main headline (perhaps just two or three words in large bold type), then an overview or lead-in to the rest of the 'story' (perhaps a sentence or two in a medium size or another colour), and then the remainder of the story in a regular body text size.

On a website there will often be no more than one 'story' to a single page, so you won't need such a large heading. This saves precious space (sometimes called 'screen real estate'), and leaves you more room to set out the story. The major heading is more likely to have its place on an earlier page, such as the home page. Your visitors will appreciate anything you can do to save them from unnecessary page jumps, and a good technique is for the contents page to feature the major headings with the lead-in paragraphs as subheadings. That way the reader has a better idea of what the page link will lead to.

Typical use of headlines and abstracts

The Web also offers possibilities that have no direct equivalent on the printed page, such as making some explanatory additional text pop up when the user points to a link or a headline. These 'hover' or 'roll-over' effects can be very attractive and save a lot of visual clutter, but you need to be sure they will be fairly obvious or your visitors may simply think you haven't provided enough detail on what's available and may move off elsewhere.

You can also use additional panels or ruled-off areas to give background to a story, or to explain a particular point (just like the coloured panels in this book). This is a good way to provide extra information to someone who wants it without interfering with the smooth flow of the main text. Web pages handle this requirement far better than the printed page by using links to subsidiary pages that have their own links back to the main story. Advanced users might even open your extra detail in a second browser window so they can refer to it alongside the main text.

CREATING AND SAVING NEW PAGES

Before you can lay out words you need a web page to hold them. Creating new pages in *FrontPage Express* is no different from starting a new document in a word processor – you simply use the **New** command from the **File** menu to start a new blank page, and save it using the **Save** command from the same menu. In the early stages, it is easiest to save all your pages in the same directory so you can refer to the files simply by their names, for example `welcome.htm`. In normal use, visitors jump from page to page by means of links and do not need to type in the file names, so you can use whatever naming style suits you as long as you stick to acceptable characters (*see the next* **Try it now** *for details*).

As well as its system file name, each web page can have a **title**. The title wording is completely independent of the file name and it can contain whatever you want (including spaces and other symbols). You don't have to enter any title text for a page, but it will be displayed in a number of important places, so it's worth taking the trouble to enter something meaningful. The current page title appears in the title bar at the top of the browser window, and it is the default name offered when a visitor adds your page to the **Favorites** list. More significantly, if someone finds your page in a **search engine** the page title is presented to them at the head of your entry in the results list. If your titles are interesting and relevant you will increase the chances of your pages being visited (*see* **Pulling the crowds**, *page 166*).

The default title inserted by *FrontPage Express* is 'Untitled normal page' which is hardly likely to spur the interest of a potential visitor! So get into the habit of entering a title every time you create a fresh page. You might also take the opportunity to add your own details as the author of the page. This information isn't routinely displayed by the browser, but is visible to anyone viewing the page source. It's entirely up to you whether or not you include your name or any contact information.

TRY IT NOW:
SETTING UP A NEW PAGE

If they aren't already running, start *Internet Explorer* and *FrontPage Express* (from here onwards, the **Try it now** sections will assume you have already started these applications). You'll see a new, blank document area and a set of toolbars looking rather like a typical word processor.

Since it starts up with usable settings for everything important, you could just type away as you would in a word processor. A few things are worth setting up before you start typing, like the page title, the basic colour scheme and your own details. Click **Page Properties** on the **File** menu (or right-click the page and choose **Properties**) to open a dialogue in which you can set the attributes of the whole page.

On the **General** tab, enter 'Welcome to Gairloch'. for the title, and on the **Background** tab set the default colours as shown here (*right*).

If you would also like to enter your details as author, go to the **Custom** tab and click **Add** beside the **User Variables** section. In the **User Meta Variable** box that appears, enter 'AUTHOR' in the **Name** box, and your own details in the **Value** box. Click **OK** to return to the **Properties** dialogue.

Our basic page style is now complete, so click **OK** to close the **Page Properties** dialogue. You should see a blank page with a maroon background and your new title showing on the title bar. You won't see the author details, but any that you entered are now in the HTML source text and you can check them by clicking HTML on the **View** menu.

Before we save this page, you might like to add a piece of standard text that will appear on most pages

Decrease text size

Text colour

to show when they were last modified. Press **Return** to start a second line (leaving the first one blank), select the **Verdana** typeface in the font drop-down, click the **Decrease Text** button three times, click the **Text Colour** button, choose an orange colour and click **OK**. Type in 'Last modified' plus the current date, and your page should look like this:

Now save the page by clicking the usual disk icon button, or clicking **Save** on the **File** menu, or using the Ctrl+S shortcut key. You can save this page with any name you like by clicking the **As File** button and navigating your filing system in the usual way. We will save it as `c:\mypages\gairloch_base.htm` to be used as a basic page from which we can develop others. The save dialogue has another reminder to enter a meaningful title if you have not already done so. If you aren't confident that you have created the file correctly, you can download the sample of the same name from the sample files on the Web.

Save

LAYING OUT THE WORDS

There are significant differences between laying out words for the printed page and laying them out on a web page. Most of these revolve around the fact that your words are effectively reformatted 'on-the-fly' when they are displayed by a visitor's web browser, and in simple HTML work you can't assume that they will look exactly as they looked when you designed the page.

In a word processor you choose type sizes in point sizes, such as 10 point for normal text or 24 point for a heading. One point is ½ inch high, so those type sizes represent actual sizes on the page. Web browsers are used on widely varying screen sizes and there is no guarantee that a particular piece of text will be shown at a given size, so standard HTML offers only relative font sizes numbered 1 to 7. The default size for 'normal' text is 3.

Browsers allow users to enlarge or reduce the overall viewing scale of text on a web page. In *Internet Explorer* there are five magnifications from smallest to largest. The browser keeps the correct relationship between the seven design sizes, but it doesn't guarantee that the text will appear at a specific height. Only users who stick to 'normal' view will see the text at the same nominal size you saw when you built the page.

Font size menu in Internet Explorer

If you don't specify a particular typeface, a PC browser will use *Times New Roman*. You can specify any face you like when designing your pages, but you must be careful, because your choice of typeface may not be available on all your visitors' computers. *See also* **Putting on the style: Typography**, *page 139*.

The browser reformats paragraphs as required for display, taking into account the window size and shape and the user's preferred text size. This raises one final point to bear in mind when writing for web pages. Your readers may be able to see only a relatively small portion of your text at a time, and may be using a browser window that's a different shape from yours. If the reader resizes the browser window then the text will be rearranged to fit the space, which means it may take up more or fewer lines on the screen. So don't place too much reliance on the text being laid out exactly as you envisaged it, or on it all being visible at once.

SPECIAL TEXT STYLES

As well as basic placement of text, standard HTML offers a few extra layout options. You can investigate these by highlighting some text in the *FrontPage* editor and, from the **Format** menu, clicking **Font**, then the **Special Styles** tab. Most of the styles shown here are described in terms of function such as **Citation** or **Definition**. The sample window will show you the normal effect of your choices. An oddity is that if you select **Bold** or **Italic** in this dialogue, they are explicitly coded as <B> or <I>, rather than being specified as named styles. Yet, if you use the **B** or **I** buttons in the main editing window, they are coded using the HTML style names `<strong>` or `<em>`.

HTML offers simple control over the horizontal placement of text across the full browser window width. By default, left alignment is used, but you can select centred or right alignment. Short lines of text are not spread out to fit (justified), so if you centre a short piece of text it will appear in the middle of the window with wide margins either side. If text appears alongside an image then it will align within the space remaining beside the image.

HTML also offers handy list formatting options – using simple bullets or sequential numbers or letters – to provide a quick, clear way to lay out short lists within the text. You can control the type of item labelling (1, 2, 3…, a, b, c…, i, ii, iii… and so on), but you can have only the default colour and size. The whole list is enclosed in a pair of HTML tags – `<UL>`*bulleted list*`</UL>` for bullets, and `<OL>`*numbered list*`</OL>` for numbered lists – and each item is enclosed in a list item tag pair – `<LI>`*item*`</LI>`.

Horizontal rules are another useful layout device built into standard HTML text coding. A horizontal rule is inserted by a simple `<HR>` code and has the useful property that it automatically reaches the full width of the browser window, whatever that may be. Rules are usually drawn with a slight relief effect, which makes them appear to be engraved in the page, and suitable vertical space is automatically added above and below.

TRY IT NOW: A BASIC TEXT PAGE

If you do not have the `gairloch_base.htm` page open, open it now (you may find it as a recent item on the **File** menu). We will use this as the basis for creating the first page of the Gairloch website. The first thing to do is to save the page under a new name, `welcome.htm`. Even though we haven't yet changed the page, it is worth saving to a new file name now to avoid any risk of overwriting our base page design.

Most of the text on the Gairloch pages will be in the *Verdana* typeface, so select that in the font selector.

Click to place the cursor at the start of the first line, and select **Heading 1 style** from the **Change Style** drop-down. Enter the first line of page text 'Welcome to Gairloch', which should appear in large yellow type. Press **Enter** to start a new paragraph, and

select **Heading 1 style** again. The next line is going to be in the Gaelic language (the traditional language of the area) and we will make it distinct. Click **Font** on the **Format** menu, select a colour of green and bold-italic style, and click **OK**.

Now type 'Fàilte gu Geàrrloch'. As you can see, this includes an accented vowel, a-grave (à), which is not on the standard British keyboard. There are various ways to generate accented characters in

Windows, but *FrontPage Express* provides a handy built-in tool for non-standard

symbols. Click **Symbol** on the **Insert** menu and you will get a chart of all the symbols available in the current character set. Select the one you want, press **Insert**, and it will be placed in the text at the cursor position. Use this to complete the line. Now start a new line and type the remaining text: 'Come on in and find out all about things to do and places to visit in the scenic beauty of Gairloch, Wester Ross.' You should have a window looking like this:

Don't worry if it's not identical – tidy it up later, or load `try-it-now-2.htm` from the sample files on the Web.

To bring in text from another application, use the usual cut-and-paste methods to avoid re-keying. Another quick way to add material from a text file is to use the **File** command on the **Insert** menu – see the next **Try it now**.

TRY IT NOW:
LISTS AND RULING LINES

To try out these HTML layout features, we'll create a basic page for attractions in the area. Open the `gairloch_base.htm` page as a starting point and re-save it as `attractions-1.htm`. Don't forget to give it a title in the **Save As** dialogue – we'll call it 'Gairloch attractions'.

Now we need to add the basic text to the page. So that you don't spend unnecessary time typing, you can load this from the `try-it-now-4.txt` file. Place the cursor at the top left of the editing window, and use the **File** command from the **Insert** menu to locate and load the text. Select **Text files** in the **Files of type** box, select the `try-it-now-4.txt` file, and click **Open**. A text conversions dialogue will come up, and you should select **Normal paragraphs** so that each paragraph of the text file is imported as a paragraph of normal HTML text.

The text will come in with the original blank line still present above it, so delete that. The text will also be in the default font or in *Courier* (depending on other settings), so the first thing to do is to select everything on the page (Ctrl+A or **Edit**, **Select All**), and choose **Verdana** in the font drop-down. You can also set some larger text for the headings: set line 1 to Heading 1 style, and lines 2 and 7 to Heading 3 style. Your page should look something like this:

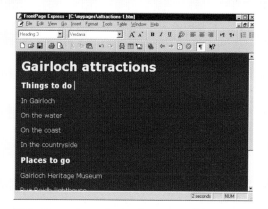

Now you are ready to try some list formatting, and the best thing to do here is experiment! Start by highlighting the four items under 'Things to do' (just as you would in a word processor), click the **Bullets** quick formatting button, and you have a neat little list formatted with bullets in just one click.

Bullets button

That's all we need for the moment, but you might like to open the **Bullets** and **Numbering** dialogue from the **Format** menu and take a look at the various options and effects available. When you have done, reset the page to use standard bullets for both lists, so it looks like this (*right*).

Horizontal ruling lines are even easier to add. Just place the cursor at the end of the paragraph immediately above where you want the horizontal rule and click **Horizontal Line** on the **Insert** menu. A gap will be opened up below the paragraph and a ruling line drawn across the width of the browser window. Try it on the main heading and you should get a result like this:

Again, experiment freely to see how this tool works. In particular, look to see what happens if you place a rule in a list section or in the middle of a line of text. In the sample web page, one rule has been placed above the lists and one below, as you can see in the sample file `attractions-1.htm`.

SIMPLE GRAPHICS

Most web pages use simple graphic elements, or '**eye candy**', to liven up the layout, provide visual markers for links to other pages, and to highlight the page title. You need to take care that these are appropriate to your subject and, as with pictures, don't use them just for the sake of it. Although they may appear to the viewer as a little button, a coloured symbol, or fancy text, they are in fact small picture files. Fortunately, they can usually be made quite a bit smaller than photos of similar dimensions because they contain less fine detail and fewer colours (*see* **Graphics files and compression**, *page 148*). It's very common to use images that give an impression of depth (for example, using **drop shadows** or **bevels**) to stand out from the two-dimensional computer screen. Although graphics are a good way to display highly decorated text, they are not a suitable way to present large amounts of text and should be used with care.

GRAPHICAL BULLETS

We have already seen that the browser can supply simple text bullets to highlight items in a list, but these can be a bit dull compared with using a small graphic image placed beside the text. Even the simplest graphical bullets can make a page more attractive by introducing a little splash of colour or shading. What's more, they can be set up to act as clickable points to jump to other pages.

A particular advantage of graphical bullets is that, even though you may use quite a few of them on one page, the bullet picture needs to be downloaded only once. The browser will re-use the same image as many times as needed on the page, and this can considerably speed up page transfer. Most WYSIWYG authoring packages come with substantial collections of bullets in matching colours and styles.

Typical bullets

GRAPHICAL BUTTONS

Visually appealing buttons, with coordinated colours, labelling and 3D shading effects, are just as easy to place on the web page as bullets. The difference between bullets and graphical buttons is that buttons are used to link to other pages or to trigger other actions. Technically there is no real difference between bullets and buttons, they are all small image files, but buttons tend to have specific text or shapes for different functions, and each unique button has to be downloaded as a separate file. Even though they are usually quite small in themselves, if you use a lot of different buttons it may noticeably increase your page loading times.

As well as visual appeal, a graphical button has an advantage over a text link in that you can easily set a small piece of descriptive text to pop up automatically when the visitor hovers over

Gairloch is in Wester Ross, Scotland

TRY IT NOW: GRAPHICAL BULLETS

In this exercise, we will replace the text bullets on the 'Attractions' page with prettier graphical bullets that will smarten up the presentation. If it isn't there already, open up `attractions-1.htm` in *FrontPage* editor. The first thing we need to do is remove the plain text bullets, so highlight the first block of bulleted text and click the bullets button again to restore the text to a set of single-line paragraphs. Do the same for the second bullet group as well.

A graphical bullet is simply a small picture file inserted in the text, so place the cursor at the start of the first list item ('In Gairloch') and click the **Insert Image** button (or choose **Image** on the **Insert** menu). Go to the **Other Location** tab and click the **Browse** button to find the sample image, `orange-bullet.gif`, then click **OK**. You could alternatively have downloaded an image from the Web with the **From Location** tab, or you could have selected it from a library of files with the clipart tab.

You will now see the bullet inserted before the text, but it is poorly placed – it's a bit too high for the text baseline. HTML offers useful alignment options to deal with this. Double-click the bullet image to open the **Image Properties** dialogue, and go to the **Appearance** tab, where you will find an **Alignment** option set to 'bottom'. If you change it to 'texttop', you will find the bullet aligns itself nicely. Before clicking **OK**, it's a good idea to turn on the **Specify Size** check box – leave the size set to its initial value of 24 x 18 pixels.

We now need to place the other six bullet images. To avoid going through the **Image Properties** dialogue again, drag copies of the first bullet into place beside each of the other text items. If you simply drag an image it will move from one place to another, but if you hold down the control key while dragging, an extra copy will be placed at the new position when you release the mouse button. You will know if you are dragging a copy if you can see the little + sign in a box beside the cursor during the operation. Be careful not to drag the re-sizing handles at the edges of the bullet;

click the mouse pointer only in the centre. Try dragging a copy now, and repeat it for each item, so you end up with a page looking like this (right):

When you are satisfied, save the page as `attractions.htm`.

the graphic. This is very useful for providing quick confirmation of the button's purpose, without the effort required to implement advanced 'hover' or 'roll-over' effects (see **Putting on the style**, *page 136*).

Most authoring programs come with collections of buttons for common purposes, for example, numbered or lettered sets for lists. They usually also include symbols for simple navigation purposes like up, down, left and right arrows, and icons for functions such as jumping to the home page, previous page or top of the current page. Using a consistent set of shapes for these purposes throughout your site has the twin benefits of providing clear 'signposts' for visitors and boosting page loading speeds. We'll see how to create the actual navigation links later.

There are many shareware and commercial software packages dedicated to generating customized buttons, based on standard designs but with your own choice of wording and colouring. Some of the authoring software and several of the online authoring systems include these utilities as part of the package (see **Candy machines**, *page 100*).

Buttons are also available in HTML forms, but these are limited to looking just like regular Windows buttons with simple text on them. They have the advantage that they can be coded entirely in simple HTML text, so there is no graphics file overhead at all. However, they can be more complicated to use and less flexible in their placement on the page.

CANDY MACHINES

There are many small software packages on the market that are dedicated to producing customized 'eye candy' – small, attractive, and usually brightly coloured graphics for use as graphical buttons, headlines or pure decoration. Most general-purpose graphics programs can also produce such items, but they often call for many steps by a practised user. The dedicated programs can take your own words or images and process them in myriad ways to apply a wide range of preset effects in seconds.

A typical good utility for this purpose is *Xara WebStyle*, which is intended for users with no special design or graphics skills, and generates images that are yours to use however you want. It provides over 1,000 templates to which you can apply your own words and style choices. A useful feature is that the templates are 'vector-based', which means they can be rescaled to generate graphics of any size without loss of quality.

Online graphics processing systems require you to buy or install no software at all. In these systems, you enter your desired text – and perhaps some style choices – into a web form. A jazzy graphic is returned to your browser a few moments later for you to save and re-use as you wish. The options available are similar to the software utilities you can buy for your own PC, but they work remotely on a server. Two systems definitely worth a look are at www.designer.com and www.zy.com.

Small, brightly-coloured graphics help to make this page attractive and eye-catching

PICTURES

You can liven up your pages even more by using pictures to illustrate what you are writing about. Apart from simply making your pages look more attractive, you will find that it really is true that 'a picture is worth a thousand words'. Not only can a picture replace a lot of words, it can also be much more quickly absorbed within your visitor's attention span.

You can also use pictures as backgrounds to your web pages, or to panels within the page. Of course, this needs some care to make sure that the text remains readable over the picture, especially at smaller type sizes. When you use a picture for a background, you can also specify a compatible alternative background colour. This ensures both that the text is readable before the picture has downloaded and that it works for visitors who have switched off pictures to speed up their browsing.

	Curtain Up
Radio on demand	Listen live from 9.35pm as t... Opera House re-opens. He Doming. Get behind the s...
	Tune in to the past
Finest hour	News bulletins, Hitler's spe... weather forecast ... experi... **voices** of World War II.
	Dirty rat's tales
See into the future.	Get a rat's eye view - take a... **down a London sewer** P the future, from archeology

Browsing with pictures disabled

Beware of using too many pictures, especially large ones. They can be very slow to download – on a web page, a picture is worth more than 1,000 bytes! Your visitors may be put off if they have to wait a long time for pictures to load, no matter how attractive the images. Again remember copyright issues – on pictures it is usually even more carefully guarded than on words.

The choice of file format and compression method will have a great influence on the speed and quality of pictures on your website, and it is worth spending some time mastering these. We will return to this topic later. For the time being it is enough to remember that most photographs and other 'real world' images are handled best for use on the Web by the **JPEG** file format, and most buttons, bullets and other graphic effects are best handled by the **GIF** format.

See also **Putting on the style**, *page 136.*

PHOTOGRAPHS AND OTHER WORKS OF ART

Local artists or photographers may be an excellent source of pictures, especially if your site is about the locality. Many will be proud to have their work shown on your site and be pleased at the additional exposure. Even so, and even though they probably won't ask for any payment, you must have their permission. If you need a lot of pictures for your topic, it might be worth getting in touch with a local amateur group or evening class organizer – you could find an eager response, leaving you spoilt for choice!

If you want to use pictures from existing prints or books, you will need to use a flat-bed scanner. This allows you to capture a digital copy of the artwork quickly and safely. You can make your own reference prints if you need paper copies to help design the pages. Avoid putting original material through a 'sheet-fed' scanner – there is too much risk of damage – and try to get material you have borrowed back to its owner as quickly as possible. You need a reputation for reliability if you want to get the best materials for any future work. Always remember that you *must* have the copyright holder's permission. Don't download someone else's work from the Web to re-use it without permission. *See also* **Copyright**, page 79.

If you want to take your own photographs for your website, a **digital camera** can be invaluable. It will let you take a lot of pictures at minimal cost, without the need for photographic processing or scanning work. You can also use a digital camera to capture images of larger printed works, such as craft work or oil paintings. You do not need an expensive camera to produce digital images of sufficient quality for the Web. The limitations of a web browser work in your favour here – you can use much lower definition pictures than you would need for good quality photographic prints.

PLACING PICTURES

Placing pictures in a web page is easy, although you may need to give some thought to sizing and positioning them to best effect. Although text may change when visitors resize the browser window, pictures do not change at all, so the size of the picture can change dramatically in relation to text areas around it. By default, the browser will show a picture at its 'natural size', measured in pixels. If you do not specify the size to be used, your page layout will jump about when pictures are loaded to the page and finally sized by the browser.

Although the browser can rescale a picture in a page to anything you specify, if you try to scale up a small image in the browser it will lose visual quality. If you scale down a large image in the browser, the quality will probably be okay, but you will waste a lot of time on transferring an unnecessarily large image file.

CLIPART AND PHOTO COLLECTIONS

Clipart is the name given to collections of images that have been produced expressly for the purpose of being incorporated in other people's work. The name refers back to its origins, which was as sheets of simple drawings, cartoon figures and so on that were designed to be cut out and incorporated in other artwork. Because clipart images are typically simple line drawings that use just a few colours and simple shapes, they can usually be saved as very small **GIF** files, which don't affect page loading times badly.

Web objects are a more recent development – small photographs of objects isolated from any original background so you can place them on your own page backgrounds. This can save many hours of trying to photograph objects against plain backgrounds and 'masking' them out in computer graphics software. Web objects are available in their own right, or as part of larger clipart collections.

Many software packages, from office software to graphic design applications, come with extensive libraries of clipart. Much of it is mediocre, but you can often find a jokey little image or set of images that is just right to liven up a plain page. If you already have office or publishing software, check it out – you may already have quite a collection of clipart. As with all these web page adornments, clipart is best used in moderation. Used to excess, it can be unbearable!

Some packages combine clipart, photographs, and even some video and sound clips, all with a licence to incorporate them in your website or other publications. *Corel Gallery* is a typical series. At the last count, the top product in this range came with over 1.3 million images, including 60,000 photographs, for under £80. Another well-known collection is Imsi's *MasterClips*

TRY IT NOW: PLACING PICTURES

We have already covered the topic of placing pictures, under the guise of inserting graphical bullets. However, pictures usually require more work on the alignment and scaling options to place them correctly in relation to the text. All images on the page are effectively anchored at a chosen point in the text. With bullets this is to be expected, as they form part of the text layout, but with larger pictures, it can be difficult to select the right combination of insertion point and alignment relative to the text. We'll follow through an example, and brighten up the welcome page along the way.

Open the `welcome.htm` page now (if you didn't complete it, use the `try-it-now-2.htm` sample), and place the text cursor at the top left corner. Press **Enter** to create a new line on which we will anchor the image. Move the cursor back to the blank top line and click the **Insert Image** button (or choose **Image** on the **Insert** menu). Use the **Browse** button to load `scotland_1.gif` from the sample files. You should now see the map of Scotland on the page, but its position relative to the text leaves a lot to be desired.

To improve this, double-click the picture and go to the **Appearance** tab. Now choose **Right** in the **Alignment** drop-down and click **OK**. Things are looking much better now, with the picture placed on the right-hand side of the window and the text rearranged to the left, although the picture is still a little small for the page.

Being a simple graphic, the picture can withstand some moderate enlargement in the browser, and if we don't modify the original file, it will load just as quickly. So double-click the image, go back to the **Appearance** tab, and click the **Specify Size** box. We will enlarge the picture by 50% – any more than that and it will start to degrade. Enter 213 wide by 390 high in the dimensions boxes (*see right*).

Now review the page in your browser. Load it up and click **Refresh** – it should look something like this:

Resize the browser window and look at the result. The browser makes a reasonable job of reformatting the text to the left of the picture across a range of window sizes. If you want your sites to look good at all times, it's vital to check how pages react to changes in window size.

series, which includes a 100,000 Webart collection for less than £30. Some websites, such as the press rooms of some commercial companies, have photographs that you can download and use for free. The quality or choice of these images is often limited, but you may be lucky in finding a good-quality relevant picture.

COMPUTER GRAPHICS

Of course, you can also use drawings and images you have created for yourself with general purpose graphics software such as *Adobe Illustrator*, *CorelDRAW* or *Corel Xara*, but you will have to export the images in a format suitable for use on the Web. The choice of format will depend on the nature and purpose of the images, but as with other pictures it is usually **GIF** or **JPEG**.

See also **Putting on the style**, *page 136*.

USING MULTIPLE PAGES

We've looked at several examples of individual web pages, and sometimes a single well-crafted page is enough to put across a worthwhile message. But in most cases you will want to create a more substantial website – a structured collection of interlinked pages covering several aspects of your subject and offering visitors the opportunity to navigate around the information to find what interests them. So, once you have gathered the information and created a few basic pages, you'll need to start linking them.

Almost any object on a web page can have a **hyperlink** (or **link** for short) associated with it to direct the

browser to display the linked item. The link will
normally specify another page that is to be retrieved and
displayed. The link contains a **URL** 'pointing' to the
target and, as you know by now, the target could be
another file on the same computer, or could come from
a web server thousands of miles away. Links may also
point to other sorts of target, such as a file to be
downloaded (*see* **Target information**, *page 110*).

SIMPLE TEXT LINKS

The simplest form of link is a piece of text that visitors
can click in order to jump to something associated with
that text. Inserting a text link is very simple, and
requires you to do little more than highlight the text
concerned and enter the required target URL. Usually
the link text is highlighted in some way to indicate the
presence of a link.

By default, HTML text links are coloured blue and
underlined on the page, but the trend nowadays is to
choose whatever distinctive style suits the design of your
page. Most browsers change the shape of the pointer
when it is over a clickable object, so visitors get good
feedback as to what is a link and what isn't.

This is where you will see the attraction of keeping all
your files in the same directory – when you enter a
target URL, all you have to key in is the basic file name
rather than disk and folder names. If you work this way,
using **relative URLs**, you will also be able to upload
your site to any folder on a web server without changes
to the link details (*see* **Going live**, *page 117*).

TARGET INFORMATION

All web page hyperlinks contain a URL pointing to a target – the resource that will be activated if the link is clicked. Most targets refer either to a file relative to the current page – for example, just `gairloch.htm` – or to a page on a web server referenced by its full URL beginning with http:// – for example, `http://www.gairloch.co.uk/gem-guide/welcome.htm`. However, targets may also point to several other types of resource or cause other actions. The other types of URL that you are most likely to meet are:

`file:filename` which specifies a file to be retrieved from your local computer file system. Be careful about this, because if you include drive or directory details and upload it to a web server, the reference may work as intended only when the page is viewed on your own machine. For local files you can use forward slashes or backslashes in the name.

`mailto:address@server` which starts the user's default e-mail program and pre-addresses a new message for the user to complete. This is a very handy way to help visitors send messages easily. You can also preset a **Subject** line by adding ?subject= to the URL. For example: `mailto: alex@gairloch.co.uk?subject=CollinsGem` `ftp://ftp-server/filename` which uses the File Transfer Protocol (FTP) to retrieve a file from an FTP server. For large files this is a more reliable transfer method than HTTP, and some files are available only by this method.

Bookmarks are individual markers within an HTML file that may be included in a target URL to cause a jump to the specified place within a page. A bookmark is specified in a URL by placing a # symbol followed by the bookmark name on the end of the file name, for example `welcome.htm#top`. A typical use is jumping to another position on the current page, such as to the top, but the jump could be directly to a marked location on any page. Note that 'bookmark' in this context is nothing to do with the Netscape term of the same name. In Netscape products it has the same meaning as 'Favorites' does in *Internet Explorer*.

PICTURE LINKS

There really is very little difference between placing links on text and placing basic links on pictures. You simply double-click the picture in the authoring software and insert a hyperlink just as for text. Clicking any part of the image in a browser will cause a jump to your specified target. Traditionally images had a blue border placed around them when they were linked, but nowadays it is more usual to rely on the browser's pointer changing to indicate the presence of a link.

More advanced authoring tools and utilities can create
image maps, which divide the image up into multiple
zones ('**hotspots**'), each of which may be associated with
a different target.

EXTERNAL LINKS

Hyperlinks on text or pictures in your website may
point to pages on other websites, and you must enter
the full external URLs in order for the target pages to
be located. Apart from that, you enter them just like
links to your own pages. If you want to test external
links while you are developing the site, your computer
will need to be online so the pages can be retrieved first
time around. However, you will probably find that,
thanks to your browser's history cache, you can go
offline again after you have visited the target pages and
they will continue to be available for some time,
possibly for several weeks of testing, depending on your
browser's history settings. This is very handy! There are
several other non-technical issues to think about when
linking to external sites not under your control (*see*
Going outside, *page 115*).

MOVING ON

Now that you have seen how pages are put together,
you may want to spend some time experimenting for
yourself before moving on. You can spend as much time
as you want editing and linking pages on your own PC
without incurring any online charges. The main thing to
remember is that you should keep a frequent check on

TRY IT NOW: ADDING HYPERLINKS

Despite the power of links, they are really very easy to add. All you have to do is highlight the text or image that must be sensitive to a click and enter the target destination, such as the URL of another page or another site.

We will connect the Gairloch Welcome page to the Attractions page using a text link, and link Attractions to the On the Coast page using a graphical bullet as a button. Load the pages concerned – `welcome.htm`, `attractions.htm` and `coast.htm` – into the editor.

Use the *FrontPage Express* Window menu to show the Welcome page and type the word 'Enter' on a new line just above the bottom horizontal rule. It doesn't matter how it is formatted, but it will probably look best for the present purpose in Heading 3 style. Now select the text, and click the **Insert Hyperlink** button (or choose **Hyperlink** on the **Insert** menu). The **Create Hyperlink** dialogue appears, allowing you to link to a file on your hard disk or the Web, or to create a new page as the target, or to link to one of the other pages currently loaded in the editor.

We want to link to one of the open pages, so go to the **Open Pages** tab and you'll see the pages available. They are listed by title, but if you click one the target file name appears in the dialogue box. Select 'Gairloch – attractions' and click **OK**.

You'll get a warning that you are linking to a local file that may not be available on the Web. This is okay as

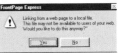

we have kept all files in one directory and are using just the file names, not drive letters or directories. As long as all the files are uploaded to one server directory all the links will work on the Web, so click **OK**.

'Enter' has been underlined to indicate it is a link, but clicking on it in the editor has no effect. To test it, save the `welcome.htm` page and switch to your browser. Load `welcome.htm` and click **Refresh** to update. Click 'Enter' and the browser should jump to Attractions.

Now we need to do the same for the Attractions page. Return to *FrontPage Express* and select the Attractions page on the Window menu. From here on, inserting the link is exactly the same as it was for the text. Click the bullet beside 'On the coast' to select it, and click the **Insert Hyperlink** button again. From the **Open Pages** tab, select the On the Coast page, and click **OK**.

Again, you will need to load the page in the browser and refresh it before you can test it. Notice that when you pass the pointer over the bullet beside 'On the coast' you will see it change to a hand pointer, and if you click it, the browser will jump directly to the coast page.

Armed with the basics of creating links, you can connect the other pages as required. What all the pages really need now is an unobtrusive, clear way for visitors to jump back to the previous or home page. Over to you!

GOING OUTSIDE

You'll almost certainly want to link to external sites from your own site, and you should give some thought to how you do it. In particular, will you link words or buttons directly wherever appropriate in your own pages, or will you collect all the external references on one page, or even have a mix of the two? This is essentially up to you and what you think will work best, but there are a few things you should consider.

Depending on what sort of site you have, particularly if it's a business one, you might want to remind visitors that the externally linked sites are beyond your control, and that you don't necessarily endorse anything on them. This can be one reason for collecting external links together on a links page, so you can place a 'disclaimer' at the head of the page.

Bear in mind that your external links are encouraging people to leave your site. You might want to remind them that they would be very welcome to return, perhaps using their **Back** button, or by adding your site to their **Favorites**. You could also mail other site owners to suggest that you insert reciprocal links to make it easy for visitors to jump back and forth. When you progress to more advanced site design, you will find ways of opening the external links in a fresh browser window so that your site stays on view as well.

how your designs look when viewed in the browser, so keep *Internet Explorer* loaded and use it to review your work. If you also have *Netscape Navigator* available it is worth using that as well so that you can see any differences in treatment of your pages between the two leading browsers. Don't forget that, to see the effect of any new changes to a page, you must save the page in the *FrontPage Express* editor *and* use the **Refresh/Reload** button (or press F5) in the browser – otherwise you will still be looking at the previous version. When you are ready to publish something to a web server on the Internet, the next section will show you what to do.

GOING LIVE

So far we have constructed a **local website**, which is a site consisting only of files on your own computer's hard disk or local network. This has two great benefits – it's fast, and you don't need to be online for the hours you might spend building and polishing your website. However, it also has the supreme disadvantage that the site can be accessed only at your computer. If you are creating a website that you want to share with the world, then sooner or later you will have to **upload** it to a web server, from where it can be viewed by anyone connected to the Internet. In this chapter you'll learn how to do that.

If you decided to use an online authoring system (*see* **Tools of the trade**, *page 29*), then your files are already present on the server and the whole 'publishing' process will probably amount to no more than clicking a single button. However, it is probably still a good idea to follow this chapter for additional tips on testing your site and so that you are aware of what's involved if you decide to develop more advanced sites at a later date.

Testing your site

Before you upload your site, do everything you can to test it out locally. It's much easier to rectify problems while the site is still on your own system, and you will avoid showing any little slips to the world! Try out every feature on every page – check that all the links work, and try things out from various starting points or in unplanned sequences. While you are doing this, keep an eye out for unnecessarily large or slow pages (*see* **Speed trials**, *page 120*).

View your pages with large and small browser windows to make sure that they look sensible when reformatted by the browser. It is also worth making the effort to install a second browser to check out your pages using both *Internet Explorer* and *Netscape Navigator*. If you go on to more advanced page design this becomes essential, as the different browsers interpret several features in slightly different ways. If you install an alternative browser just for checking, do not accept its setup invitation to make it become the default browser or you may find it jumping in when you want to do routine work with your regular browser.

INTERNAL LINKS

If you have followed the advice in the previous chapter and used relative file references (such as `welcome.htm`), not **absolute** references (such as `c:\mypages\welcome.htm`), for links within your own site, you should have no problems when the site is uploaded. If your whole site is stored in one folder it should be particularly straightforward, as all files will be referred to simply by the filename, with no drive or folder details.

Even if you have used folders (subdirectories), things will be okay as long as you have stuck to relative naming (for example, referring to an image file `picture.gif` in subfolder `images` as just `images/picture.gif`, without any drive letter or higher level folder names). This is because all the filenames will be stored relative to the current page, and it doesn't matter if the site is moved to another system so long as the folder structure is preserved during upload.

If you use absolute file references, for example `c:\mypages\welcome.htm`, the files will no longer be accessible when uploaded to a server that has no access to the hard disk on your computer. Be very careful when testing, because such links *will*, of course, work for you (and you alone), since your browser *does* have direct access to your drive C.

A good way to test for potential filename problems is to rename temporarily the top-level folder in which you have stored your website files (for example, rename `c:\mypages` as `c:\testpages`), and check out the site again. As long as you have used only relative file naming, it should all still work fine. As an extra check that you haven't referred directly to files stored outside your intended directories, you could also move the files to another computer and check it again.

EXTERNAL LINKS

If your site has links to other sites, it's particularly important to check them carefully – visitors do not appreciate wasting time on **broken links**. You can check for them while your website is still local – just go online with your browser and try them all in turn. This is easier if you have adopted the scheme of collecting your external links together on one page, since you won't have to jump all over your site to check the links. Some advanced authoring tools and online site analysis tools (*see* **Troubleshooting**, *page 133*) can carry out these checks automatically and report back on problems, but for sites with only a few links you can check things out for yourself using just your browser.

SPEED TRIALS

Your site will respond much more quickly while you are browsing it locally than it will when delivered across the Internet. So, beware of accepting slow page loading while you are testing it out offline – it will probably be several times slower online. All the same, offline page loading times will give you a good idea of the relative speeds of different pages and let you spot potential troublemakers. If a page seems slow offline it is likely to be a real drag online and you should consider doing something about it, such as splitting up the page, reducing the size of pictures, or using better compression (*see* **Putting on the style**, *page 136*).

A very useful feature of some authoring systems is a readout of expected online page loading time,

FrontPage Express's *download time indicator.*

calculated from the size of the page with all its associated files and typical Internet connection speeds. In some packages you need to use a specific command to read out the anticipated page loading time, but in the *FrontPage Express* editor it is displayed continuously by default in the bottom right status bar area. If you develop the habit of keeping an eye on this indicator while building your pages, you should be able to avoid any unpleasant surprises when testing the site!

Uploading your site

Until you have done it for the first time, this key stage in publishing your site can seem fraught with technicalities. In fact, once you have entered the necessary details on your system it is no harder than sending an e-mail or using a browser. As mentioned earlier in this chapter, if you are using an online website editing system your files will already be present on a server and they will be published for you at the click of a button. If you are using an authoring tool or text editor on your own PC, however, there is a little more effort required to transfer your website files to the web server.

If you are writing your web pages with a text editor, you will need to use a specialist FTP program to upload your files. Common examples of suitable software are *Cute-FTP*, *WS-FTP* and *Windows Commander*. These are all available as downloadable shareware, and there is usually at least one FTP program on any good computer magazine cover disk. If you are using an authoring software program, it is generally easier to use the uploading facilities that come as part of the package. Some, such as *FrontPage Express* and *Netscape Composer*, provide their own uploading systems, while others supply an independent FTP uploading application, such as *WS-FTP*, which is included with *HoTMetaL Pro*.

Internet Explorer 5 installs an additional component, the *Web Publishing Wizard*, which is dedicated to making it easy to upload to a web server without getting bogged down in the technicalities. A particularly useful feature is that the publishing wizard will try to detect the correct uploading method automatically and will configure itself accordingly. It will also remember these settings for future sessions with the same server (*see* **Using the Web Publishing Wizard**, *page 125*). *Netscape Composer* has a built-in **Publish** command on the **Tools** menu. It is less automated than Microsoft's wizard, but it is the most convenient if you are using *Netscape Composer* to create your web pages.

PREPARATION

Whichever uploading software you are going to use, there are a few essential pieces of information you will need to gather: the upload method, the upload address, a log-in name and password.

Upload method

Most web servers support two upload methods, **Hypertext Transfer Protocol** (**HTTP**) and **File Transfer Protocol** (**FTP**). A few also provide proprietary methods to work with particular authoring software.

HTTP is the method you have already come across in your browser as the standard way to retrieve pages from a web server, but on many servers it can also be used in reverse to upload pages. If your server and authoring software support HTTP, you will probably find it the simplest to use. There are some technical limitations to this method, but if it works there is no reason not to use it.

FTP is an older and more widely supported method on almost all servers, and some hosts permit only FTP for uploading. On some servers you will receive a specific log-in name and password to use for FTP operations.

UPLOAD ADDRESS

This is the server address to which your files will be transferred for publishing. If you are using HTTP, this will simply be your intended website URL. It may include subfolder names if you are publishing to a specific section of a website or server, or are sharing a server with other users, for example `www.gairloch.co.uk/collins-gem`. There may be a different, but related, address to use for FTP uploads, for example `ftp.gairloch.co.uk/collins-gem`. Your web files folder may be accessed under a longer path using FTP than it is when accessed from a browser. For example, the FTP address equivalent to the HTTP example folder above could well be `ftp://ftp.gairloch.co.uk/htdocs/collins-gem`.

LOG-IN NAME AND PASSWORD

To prevent unauthorized users from uploading files to your server area, you will have chosen a log-in name and password (or they may have been assigned for you) when you signed up for your web server space. If your web space is being provided by the same ISP as you use for Internet access, your uploading log-in name and password will usually be the same as those you use for your dial-up connection.

A good service provider will have given you all the necessary information at the time you signed up. If you are in any doubt about these details, contact your web server provider. If HTTP uploading is allowed directly to your web URL (as it is on most systems), then all you need to know are your log-in name and password.

Typical upload information supplied by an ISP

USING THE WEB PUBLISHING WIZARD

Since we used *FrontPage Express* as our sample authoring tool earlier, we will take a closer look at using its *Web Publishing Wizard* to upload our sample site. The wizard is opened from the Windows **Start** menu, not from within *FrontPage Express*, and it will take you through a series of simple steps to complete the task. After each step you can press **Next** to go on, or **Back** to retrace your steps and change your answers if necessary.

Starting the Publishing Wizard

PRELIMINARIES

First of all, the wizard will ask you to identify the files or folders you want to upload. For a new site, you will usually give the drive letter and directory name of the folder in which you have stored your website files, or the top-level folder of a folder/subfolder structure. If you have used subfolders, tick the 'Include subfolders' box. You can also specify the name of a single file to upload, perhaps when you have just revised the wording of a single page. If you don't want to type in the name directly, click the

Specifying the folder to be published

appropriate browse button and go to your file or folder in the usual way. In our example site, the folder to be uploaded is `c:\mypages`. When you are ready, click **Next**.

The wizard will now ask for a title for this website. This is not a title that is stored on the site or shown to anyone else; it is simply used as a memorable name under which to store the details for re-use the next time you upload to the same website. The first time you publish to a new site, click the **New** button and enter a descriptive name.

On future occasions, you will be able to select the correct site name at this stage and the wizard will be immediately ready to publish your work.

Naming the new web server

If you have entered a new site name, the wizard will next ask what uploading method to use. You will see there are several special methods offered in addition to

Choosing your connection method

HTTP and FTP. If you know which method your server requires select it, otherwise select 'Automatically detect'. The wizard will test the server before uploading and try to make the correct choice. Now click **Next**.

The wizard now asks for the server address and which local directory should be associated with that address on future occasions. The associated local directory is normally the 'top-level' folder on your hard disk that you want to correspond to the uploading URL you have given (in our example, `c:\mypages` will correspond to `www.gairloch.co.uk/collins-gem`). It is important to set this correctly, as it will be used during uploads of single files or folders to this web server on future occasions, in order to place them in the correct relative positions.

Specifying the upload URL and corresponding local folder

Uploading

Click **Next** when you are ready and the wizard will start the publishing process. If you are on a dial-up connection and you are not already online, your usual

Dial-up Networking connection will be started to log on to your ISP and upload the pages. Your web server will probably demand an additional log-in and password for uploading, and a dialogue box will pop

Entering your log-in name and password

up to request these. You can tick the box for these details to be remembered and automatically entered in future, but bear in mind that this is a security risk, especially if you regularly share your PC.

If you have entered all the details correctly, the wizard will now upload your files to the server and indicate whether it succeeded or failed. If it fails, it is most likely because of some simple error in the server name, log-in name or password that you entered. In this case, re-run the wizard, re-entering the relevant details carefully. Once everything is right you will get a notice of successful completion.

Congratulations – you are now a web publisher!

Checking your site online

Now your site is actually available to the world, you should check out the 'visitor experience' as thoroughly online as you did offline. The process is basically the same as checking it offline, exercising every aspect of the site under various conditions. However, there are a couple of extra things to beware of when you check it online. In particular, your results can be greatly affected by various bits of web trickery that are used to speed up normal browsing.

MULTIPLE SERVERS

Large web-hosting sites often use multiple web servers to spread the load and provide faster response to browsers. Each server contains a copy of all the websites being hosted, and browser requests are directed to whichever is the least busy server at any moment. As a user you will be unaware of these automatic processes since all the servers respond to the same name, but when you upload new files there may be a time delay before they are replicated automatically to all the servers in a group. The delay varies, but could be anything up to an hour on some systems. There may also be an intentional delay to allow for security checks or authorization of new pages.

So if you upload files and immediately go to test them, you may not be able to find them for a while. Don't panic! Wait for five minutes and try again, several times if necessary. If you find these delays unacceptably long, contact the server administrator or helpdesk. There is usually a special alternative address you can use to access the initial upload server directly, so you can review your pages even before they have had time to be replicated.

CACHES

Another side effect arises from **cache** systems used to hold temporary copies of recently requested pages for faster delivery. The cache may be at the server site, somewhere along the route, or on your own computer (maintained by the browser itself). A cache is often also included as part of a security device known as a **proxy server**, which is used by ISPs and corporate networks as protection against unwanted infiltration from outside Internet users.

If you upload an amended page and immediately try to review it on the Web, you may receive a cached copy of the old version. All you have to do is click the **Refresh/ Reload** button in your browser and a request will be sent out for a fresh copy of the page, which should be delivered independently of the caches.

Even your own computer maintains a local cache of recent pages – *Internet Explorer* calls these **Temporary Internet files**. These are what allow you to step back through pages you have recently visited, even after you have disconnected from the Internet. If you are trying to assess the realistic speed of your pages on the Web, you need to be wise to the effects of the local cache. Its whole purpose is the rapid delivery of pages you have already visited by reading temporary copies from your local system rather than fetching them across the Internet. So, with normal cache settings you will see realistic loading speeds only on the first visit to each page, or by pressing **Reload** on each page.

The 'temporary' files may remain on your system for days or even months. However, you can alter your browser settings to control the use of the local cache and specify when the browser will decide to check for new copies of a page it already has in the cache. In *Internet Explorer*, the settings are in **Tools/Internet Options/General/Temporary Internet Files**. In *Netscape Navigator*, they are in **View/Preferences/Advanced/Cache**. If you want, you can completely disable the local cache, but remember to reset it afterwards if you want to return to normal speedy viewing of the Web for general browsing.

If you checked everything carefully offline, uploaded successfully and checked everything online, you should now have a fully functional basic website. If you find problems, even making allowances for caches and so on, follow through the tips in the **Troubleshooting** panel. It takes a good deal longer to read about the process of uploading your site than it will usually take you to do it, and you will soon find it as easy as checking your e-mail. Once you have mastered the basics of creating a site and uploading it, you can start to think about maintaining and altering the site (*see* **Maintaining your site**, *page 178*), and creating more advanced pages with special features to put across your message more effectively (*see* **Putting on the style**, *page 136*).

TROUBLESHOOTING

If your site worked fine when it was on your local hard disk but now doesn't work properly when viewed across the Web, it is usually down to some very simple little error that isn't obvious at first. Read through the following likely causes of problems, then check the corresponding details of your site and the upload procedure carefully.

Navigation problems are usually caused by:

● failure to upload all the required files – this is most likely to happen if you have uploaded the site 'manually' using FTP, or if you entered the wrong folder names in the publishing dialogues

● using mixed uppercase and lowercase letters in filenames or links (for example, using `welcome.htm` and `Welcome.htm`) – your browser doesn't mind, but the web server probably does

● using an absolute reference in a link, such as `/mypages/welcome.htm` – the corresponding folder on the server is probably called something completely different

● using inconsistent file name endings, for example `welcome.htm` and `welcome.html` – this is unlikely to happen, though, if you are using an authoring tool correctly

For more information on these points, refer back to **Building your site**, *page 72*. Ask friends to review your site from their own computers – they may spot problems that you have not. For example:

● unsuitable fonts, such as ones that are on your system but not always installed on other people's

● non-'**web-safe**' colours, causing unpleasant **dithering** effects for visitors who use 256-colour display settings

● navigation failures from the use of a local reference in a link, such as `c:\mypages\welcome.htm`

Feedback from friends should also alert you to anything that doesn't work as you intended from a style or layout point of view – take note of their comments and see what you can do to improve things. There's more advice on the use of fonts and colour in **Putting on the style**, *page 136*.

ADVANCED CHECKS

If you can't see why a particular page is failing, or you want a thorough independent technical assessment of your web pages, you can use various online site checkers or HTML validation systems. These will go through your web pages looking for anything that doesn't meet strict HTML standards or that may not work reliably in all situations.

Don't be too alarmed if a page that looked fine throws up all sorts of comments and potential problems in a checker – with some of the more advanced validators, it can be difficult to sift the important points from the mass of minor technical infringements that crop up. The chances are that most of the items reported will have no significant effect, and most validators will indicate the relative severity of problems. There is an excellent list of such tools in the *Yahoo!* directory at `dir.yahoo.com/Computers_and_Internet/Information_and_Documentation/Data_Formats/HTML/Validation_and_Checkers/`.

PUTTING ON THE STYLE

The most effective and enjoyable web pages are those that have the best combination of content and style. Of course, the quantity and complexity of content and the appropriate styling vary dramatically. It's often the case that a page strong on content will demand a simple style, and a page with very advanced styling may have little factual content. In this, the Web is no different from paper publishing – just compare the styling and content used in a telephone directory to that used in a fashion magazine.

We have already seen that there are severe technical restraints on fancier web pages that use pictures, mainly related to file sizes and downloading speeds. However, with care it is possible to achieve impressive results with minimal file sizes, and in this chapter you will see what practical options there are for livening up pages and adding all sorts of resources and effects that are simply impossible in conventional print.

Writing

Your actual writing style is not limited by the Web, but you should still take account of browser presentation when writing or editing material provided by others. We've already looked at the importance of matching your writing to your readers – you would write differently for eight-year-olds than you would for adults – but you may also need to adapt your style for better effect on the Web.

A web page presents considerably fewer words at a time than a page in a book or newspaper, and the reader's eye is invariably tempted to stray to attractive images elsewhere on the screen. So your writing generally needs to be crisp and direct to keep the reader's interest. Compared with printed texts, writing for the Web works better with short sentences and with less complex structures.

Of course, some people will be seeking detail and will have the motivation to read longer passages of text, or even to print them out for later reading. This is where you can play to the strengths of the Web by providing unlimited pages of additional material at the click of a button or keyword, without obscuring your main message or diverting the attention of a casual reader.

If you have a lot of supporting material to present, think carefully about how to make it available in a consistent but unobtrusive fashion. For example, you might have explicit cross-reference links, such as 'click here for more details', or you might simply make keywords or phrases clickable items within the text. The explicit links are less likely to be overlooked by the reader, but they may interrupt the flow of your writing. A third possibility is to introduce a small set of unobtrusive graphical markers that indicate various sorts of supporting material.

As with all aspects of your website, try to put yourself in a visitor's place and review your material with an open mind. Look for ways in which it might be accidentally misread or confusing, and reword things to avoid the problems. Ideally, test out your material on appropriate readers who have not been involved in its production and take note of their reactions.

Typography

The Web's coding language, HTML, was originally
developed for online scientific and technical papers, so
it's hardly surprising that the first version was well
suited to book-style presentation of facts, figures and
diagrams, with design support only for straightforward
and consistent (some might say boring) layout.
However, when it comes to the dramatic and stylish use
of different fonts, flexible placing, and orientation of
text and use of colour, the typographic limitations of
basic HTML are all too obvious. The original HTML
has been steadily revised and extended through HTML
2 and HTML 3.2 to HTML 4, largely to address the
demands of designers for more flexibility and control
over layout.

The vigorous development of the language has been a
blessing and a curse – not all browser manufacturers
introduced support for new features at the same time,
and the 'standards' have been forced to adopt various
extensions after they had already come into use. Great
efforts have been made to try to maintain compatibility
with the old systems, but not always with complete
success. This means that you have to take some care
when introducing fancy new features to your website,
as users of older browsers may see a badly distorted
version of what you intended, or see nothing at all.

Fortunately, things have become a bit more settled, and
on most websites you can be sure that most of your
visitors will be using a browser that supports all the

official facilities of HTML 4 (that is, they will be using version 4 or later of *Internet Explorer* or *Netscape Navigator*). Only you can decide how much account you need to take of older browsers – even 1% of web users working with *Internet Explorer 3*, for example, can still amount to a lot of people.

ACCESSIBILITY

Just as with 'real-world' visitor facilities, you should give careful thought to designing pages that will be accessible to people with disabilities, particularly those with impaired vision who may be using unusual screen sizes and colours, or even using Braille or voice-reading equipment. There is a good selection of links with more information on this topic at the US Center for Information Technology Accommodation: see `www.itpolicy.gsa.gov/cita`. *See also* **A critical eye on your code**, *page 35*.

STYLE SHEETS

HTML itself was never intended to provide fine control over placement, colour or typefaces – it describes the structure of documents (headings, paragraphs, lists and so on), and leaves the layout details to the browser. Some designers and authoring tools pull a lot of complex tricks with HTML code to achieve the effects they want, but the non-standard code that results can cause a lot of problems for unusual browsers or special equipment. Care should be taken when utilising such effects in your design.

Cascading style sheets tackle this issue head on by separating the coding of the text from the text styles that will be used for each code. For example, most browsers interpret the <EM> tag (emphasis) as italic, but your style sheet could override this and specify that it should be bold italic. The style sheet would specify this in the following manner:

```
<style type="text/css">
  em { font-style: italic; font-weight: bold; }
</style>
```

With that style in force, wherever the <em> tag is applied the text will appear as bold italic. Style sheets also let you name your own mark-up styles for special purposes. A useful spin-off from this is that if you want to change the way all occurrences of a particular style are displayed, you need change it only once in the style sheet. Even better, you can develop a style sheet that applies to a whole website, with each page linked to it. In this way you build in a consistency of style throughout the site and can make site-wide style changes relatively easily.

Pages using style sheets are displayed properly only in version 4 or later browsers (and even then there are differences between various browsers). A detailed coverage of style sheets would need a whole book in itself, and they are generally used only with the aid of advanced authoring tools, but it's worth learning more about them if advanced typography and layout are important to you.

ADOBE ACROBAT

If you need to deliver a faithful reproduction of a single- or multi-page document such as a promotional brochure, including specific fonts and advanced design, then **Adobe's Portable Document Format (PDF)** offers a widely supported alternative. PDF files contain all the text, graphics and font information needed to reproduce the document accurately, but optimized and compressed to make the smallest possible file.

Anyone wanting to view or print a PDF document must install the *Adobe Acrobat Reader*, which is available as a free download from www.adobe.com, or as a free utility on many magazine cover disks. The reader is available as a standalone application, or as a browser plug-in to view PDF documents directly in the browser window. The user can move between pages, zoom in on accurate detail and reprint pages (unless you disable this option), but they cannot edit the document.

Although the reader software is free, to produce a PDF document in the first place you need to buy the *Adobe Acrobat Exchange* program, or a much cheaper UK alternative, *5D PDF Creator* from 5D Solutions (www.five-d.com). A PDF file can be generated from any Windows application that can print through the standard Windows printing system, and you can trade off compression against quality to suit the final purpose.

OTHER TYPOGRAPHIC OPTIONS

If it is important for you to use specific fonts on a web page and you cannot guarantee that they will be installed on visitors' computers, you can use **font embedding**. However, this requires work to prepare a font (using a free tool from Microsoft), and it is not universally supported.

A simpler option is to use the FONT FACE tag's facility to specify 'fall back' alternatives. For example, if you want to use the *Verdana* font, but you are not sure it will be available on the visitor's system, you can specify something like:

```
<FONT FACE="Verdana,Arial,Geneva,Helvetica">
```

This will use *Verdana* if possible, otherwise it will use *Arial* if that is available, on a Macintosh it will probably use *Geneva*, and otherwise it will use *Helvetica*. In the unlikely event that the system has none of those fonts, it will revert to the browser's default font (usually *Times*).

In order to make a wider variety of fonts available on all systems, Microsoft distributes a free set of core web fonts including *Comic Sans*, *Verdana*, *Impact* and *Georgia*, installed with *Internet Explorer* and various other Microsoft applications, and available for free download. You can find out more about typography on the Web and obtain the free web fonts from www.microsoft.com/typography.

Using colour

It's hard to imagine the Web without colour, yet that's how it started out in the early 1990s. At that time, it was common for personal computers to use displays capable of only 16 or 256 colours on screen at a time, with no more than 640 × 480 pixels. Nowadays, web pages revel in colour and many visitors' computers can display 16.7 million colours at high resolution.

HTML lets you specify any of the 16.7 million colours for text, ruling lines and backgrounds. However, if your page is viewed on a 256-colour system, almost all of these colours will be '**dithered**' – simulated by fine dot patterns mixing other colours available in the 256-colour range – and will be degraded. So, it's still wise to design your pages to look good on a 256-colour display as far as you can. To make this easy, browsers define a standard set of 216 '**browser-safe**' colours that will display cleanly on 256-colour displays.

SPECIFYING COLOURS IN HTML

The 'true-colour' 16.7 million colour range is created by every combination of 256 shades of red, green and blue available on a personal computer. A small selection of colours can be specified by name ('red', 'yellow', and so on), but this is impractical for the full range, and most shades are defined by a numbering system instead. The numbering system is hexadecimal (base 16), which is not easy for the beginner to use. Fortunately, if you are using an authoring tool, all you have to do is pick colours in the usual way from an on-screen palette and the corresponding code will be inserted for you.

The 216 browser-safe colours are composed of every combination of six evenly spaced shades of red, green and blue. There are standard names for all of them, but many of the names are contrived ('BlanchedAlmond', 'NavajoWhite', and so on), so it is better to stick to the colour picker for these as well.

You can apply a colour attribute to text font tags and horizontal rules. For example, a change to red text is coded as `<FONT COLOR="Red">`, and a blue horizontal rule would be `<HR COLOR="Blue">`. Of course, in a WYSIWYG editor you can simply select the item in question and choose a colour from the colour palette or drop-down.

You can also specify colours in the `<BODY>` tag, which has five colour attributes that affect the whole page:

BGCOLOR=	Controls page background colour
TEXT=	Controls the default colour of page text
LINK=	Controls the colour of unvisited hyperlinks
ALINK=	Controls the colour of a hyperlink just clicked
VLINK=	Controls the colour of previously visited hyperlinks

To achieve its colour scheme, the code for our `gairloch.htm` page included:

```
<body bgcolor="#800000" text="#FFFF00"
link="#FFFFFF" vlink="#008000" alink="#00FF00">
```

These numbers were inserted by the *FrontPage Express* editor, but we could have put them in by hand as:

```
<body bgcolor="Maroon" text="Yellow"
link="white" vlink="Green" alink="Lime">
```

which is a good deal easier for a human to read!

Colours can also be specified in the `<TABLE>` tag, using BGCOLOR= to set a background colour to the table and BORDERCOLOR= to set the colour of the cell divider lines. Note that, in a typical minor incompatibility, *Netscape Navigator* does not support these attributes.

Graphics

In this section we will look at some more advanced aspects of using graphics to liven up your site. In essence this is very simple, as we saw earlier in **Building your site**, *page 72*. In a WYSIWYG authoring tool, you simply place the cursor where you want the graphic and use the appropriate **Insert** command. In HTML coding, a picture is inserted with the <IMG> tag. For example, the Scotland map is inserted in the `gairloch.htm` page with the following HTML code:

```
<img src="scotland_1.gif" alt="Gairloch is in
Wester Ross, Scotland" align="right"
width="214" height="390">
```

Note the use of the `alt=` attribute. This specifies alternative text that will be used as a placeholder when the graphic is not visible. It's important to enter meaningful text here to help visitors with disabilities or those using very slow phone lines.

BITMAP FILES

A bitmap image is simply a collection of regularly spaced rows of coloured dots known as **pixels**, and all modern web browsers support 'bitmap' image files stored in the **GIF**, **PNG** or **JPEG** format (*see* **Graphics files and compression**, *page 148*). You may already be familiar with handling these images from a camera or scanner using image-editing software such as *PaintShop Pro*, *Adobe PhotoShop* or *Corel PhotoPaint*.

GRAPHICS FILES AND COMPRESSION

Pictures for reproduction directly on your web page must be stored in a format that is recognized by browsers or the image will not appear on the page. The file format affects two important aspects of your images: how many unique colours they may contain and how well they are 'compressed' to reduce the file size needed for a given image without spoiling it.

Graphics programs generally offer a wide range of export formats to choose from, including the two main formats suitable for the Web, **GIF** and **JPEG**, and it is usually fairly easy to decide which is most appropriate for a particular image. You can use other special graphics formats for advanced purposes, with the aid of a **plug-in** or other viewing software, but we are concerned here with simple in-page images, including the likes of photos, buttons and clipart.

GIF files may contain a maximum of 256 unique colours out of a choice of 16.7 million, while JPEG files may contain any or all of the 16.7 million (also known as 24-bit colour). This means that GIFs can reproduce graphical objects such as bullets and buttons, which have just a few shades of one or two colours, but JPEGs are needed for images with a large range of colours, such as photographs. GIF is also better at compressing simple graphics, while JPEG is better at compressing photos or similarly detailed images. So the overall choice is fairly easy:

● use GIF for graphic shapes, screenshots and diagrams, especially simple shapes or large areas of similar colour

● use JPEG for photos, paintings or other images with lots of colour variation or 'real world' detail

GIF's compression method doesn't degrade the image at all – it reproduces exactly what was saved (lossless compression). In JPEG you can choose how strongly the compression is applied, and the stronger the compression, the more the image is degraded (lossy compression). Photos can often be compressed by a factor of up to 50 before the picture is degraded too much for web display. This speeds up page loading substantially.

GIF files can also contain simple animated bitmap graphic sequences (*see* **Multimedia**, *page 156*). Another format designed specifically for the Web, Portable Network Graphics (PNG), offers the lossless compression qualities of GIF with the 24-bit colour range of JPEG, but it is not yet widely used.

The main issue with bitmap images is that they have a fixed definition, based on the number of pixels across and down the image. If a bitmap is viewed at a suitable size, the individual pixels cannot be distinguished and a smooth, clear image is seen. If you try to scale up a small bitmap image, the pixels will become obvious and spoil the picture. So, the bigger you want to present an image the more pixels it will need to remain clear, which in turn implies a larger file.

If pictures are important to your site and you want visitors to be able to see them in best quality, a useful technique is to include a small, fast image for reference, and set it up as a link to a much larger version of the same image. Your visitors can browse the smaller 'thumbnail' images quickly and you can include more of them on a page without unacceptable loading times. The larger images are there for those who think they are worth waiting for, and can be as large as you think sensible. You can include a simple jump-back link from the enlarged images, or you can advise visitors to use the browser's **Back** button to return to the thumbnails.

FILE COMPRESSION AND OPTIMIZATION

Because of the problems of handling large image files in all types of publishing, a lot of work has been done on file **compression** techniques and specialized file formats that can dramatically reduce bitmap file sizes and transfer times (see **Graphics files and compression**, *page 148*). But it still remains true that, in any given format, the larger the picture, the larger (and slower) the file will be.

If you are working with lots of pictures, or with necessarily large pictures, you should try using graphics **optimization** software. These applications try to determine the minimum amount of detail that needs to be retained, the maximum amount of compression that may be applied to an image based on the content of the graphic, and your intended use – file sizes can sometimes be reduced dramatically.

Ulead's *SmartSaver Pro* is a good example of low-cost image optimization software. It can slim down GIF, JPEG and PNG format files, and has an automated batch mode for unattended processing of large sets of files. It may also be used as a 'plug-in' within *Adobe Photoshop*, *PaintShop Pro* or *Corel PhotoPaint*.

IRREGULAR SHAPES AND TRANSPARENCY

Bitmap files contain rectangular images, and web browsers place graphics as rectangles on screen. For straightforward diagrams and photographs this is just what you want, and if the background of your image is the same as the web page background (say, white), then everything will look fine. At other times you may have an unusual colour – or indeed another image – in the background, and you may not want a contrasting rectangle to appear around your images as will happen by default.

You can fix this problem using the **transparency** feature of GIF and PNG files. This allows you to specify that pixels of a chosen colour should be displayed as transparent. If you surround your graphic with this colour, whatever is in the background of the browser page will show through and the graphic will appear to have been cut-out and placed on the web page. You can also use the transparent colour within the graphic to create pierced effects.

Bitmap editors that can save GIF files offer control over what colour will be assigned as transparent. It is common to want to use white for a transparent surround and yet also need it as an opaque colour within a graphic. This is no problem as there can be more than one occurrence of the same colour in the 256-colour GIF palette, but you need to take some care as to which white is white and which is transparent while you are drawing!

ANTI-ALIASING

Good bitmap editors also offer a technique known as 'anti-aliasing', in which the edges of bitmap shapes are surrounded with graduated shades of pixel that give the visual effect of a smoother edge when viewed at a distance. This is very widely used for web graphics, but you must be careful about what background colour has been selected when the anti-aliasing is applied. If, for example, you anti-alias a graphic with yellow as the transparent surround colour, and then place it on a blue background page, you will see a fringe of faded yellow pixels around the object. To avoid this, you must set the object's surrounding to a similar colour to the eventual background page before it is anti-aliased.

IMAGE MAPS

Bitmap images divided into clickable regions ('**hotspots**') can provide a very attractive and intuitive means of navigation. Sometimes the image can be presented rather like a map (it may indeed be a map, for example on a travel site to allow the user to click a region of interest) or it might be composed of individual clickable items separated by transparent regions.

Regions of an image are marked out by `area=` attributes that specify rectangles, circles or arbitrary polygons, and indicate the URL to jump to when the visitor clicks in that area. The HTML codes for these areas are:

```
<area shape="rect" coords="left-x,top-y,
right-x,bottom-y" href=URL>
<area shape="circle" coords="centre-x,
centre-y,radius" href=URL>
<area shape="poly" coords="x1,y1,x2,y2,x3,y3…"
href=URL>
```

The x and y positions refer to the pixel numbers in the image, starting at the top left with x=0 and y=0.

We can add a clickable area to the Scotland map on the sample website to indicate the Wester Ross area of the Highlands, and use it to jump to information about Wester Ross. The picture here shows the selection tool

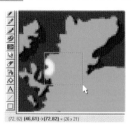

being used in *PaintShop Pro* to determine the coordinates of the required area (highlighted in blue on the status bar). Most image editing tools will show you a readout of the x, y position of the cursor as you move it around on the image, but it can still be very tedious to transfer the coordinates manually, especially with polygons. Fortunately many WYSIWYG authoring packages include tools for generating the HTML code automatically as you draw and edit image areas. Here is the code for the Wester Ross area:

```
<map name="scotland_1_map">
   <area shape="rect" coords="46,61,70,82"
   href="wester-ross.htm" alt="Wester Ross">
</map>
```

More code is required to complete the use of an image map, but this shows the essential idea. Several shareware applications, such as *Meracl ImageMap Generator* (http://come.to/meracl/), are dedicated to defining image map areas and generating the corresponding HTML code.

VECTOR GRAPHICS

In contrast to bitmaps, **vector graphics** are composed of lines, curves, outlines and fills specified in numerical terms. This has the big advantage of being 'resolution independent', in other words a vector image can be scaled up or down with no loss of quality. This sort of representation is ideally suited to graphs, mechanical diagrams, street maps and so on. Unfortunately, web browsers do not directly support any form of vector graphics presentation.

Many proprietary plug-in viewers are available which allow browsers to display vector graphics. A good example is the web plug-in available for viewing *Xara Webster* files (available from www.xara.co.uk). This can display amazingly compact .web format vector graphic files in a browser window, and viewers can pan around the image and zoom in to great magnification with no loss of quality. The images can include advanced effects such as transparency, and a complex drawing can often be reduced to just a few kilobytes. Of course, the disadvantages are that you need to buy the *Xara Webster* or *Corel Xara* programs to generate the .web format files in the first place, and your visitors need to download the 250Kb browser plug-in (but once only).

Multimedia

In web terms, multimedia generally refers to presenting dynamic content such as audio, video and graphic animations. Technically it is generally quite straightforward to do this with modern PCs and browsers, but the file size problems that arise with bitmap graphics become even greater. Typical web video, even running at only six frames per second, is effectively presenting six bitmap graphics every second, so you can see how the file downloading requirements could multiply. Similarly, even moderate quality sound recordings take typically 5Kb of data per second, and good quality can demand many times more.

Some excellent advances have been made in multimedia encoding and compression techniques, even more so than with still images, and the latest formats can achieve remarkable results. Video in particular is very compressible, as most frames are quite similar to the previous one, so it is possible to encode just the differences from frame to frame with great savings in file size. But the files are still large in comparison with text and still pictures, so you need to make sure that they are used to good effect, not just for the sake of it.

Even early browsers running under Windows can handle audio and video files in the standard Windows file formats of .wav and .avi, but these large files (anything up to 10Mb for one minute of CD-quality audio) must be downloaded in their entirety before the visitor hears or sees anything. To overcome this problem, several **streaming** formats have been developed in which playback can start while the file is still downloading. With a fast modem line, indefinite sound or video replay of moderate quality can be achieved. The best-known streaming audio format is **RealAudio**. If you want to include streamed audio or video in your website, you will need to pick a web server host that supports this – many do not. Your host service provider should be able to provide you with all the information needed to upload and use streaming audio or video.

If your site relies heavily on audio or video replay, you should consider providing a support page to help visitors deal with technical difficulties. And remember that in all cases you must make sure that you have the copyright holder's permission to reproduce recordings and pictures (*see* **Copyright**, *page 79*).

PLUG-INS

As with vector graphics, multimedia effects generally rely on browser plug-ins or other supporting components to present the material. However, multimedia is such a widespread requirement that the current browsers come complete with software to handle a wide range of common formats, including standard Windows video and sound files, MIDI music and Apple *QuickTime* files. The *Internet Explorer 5* installation screen shows the very wide range of components now shipping as standard. Anyone without these multimedia components can download them from

Microsoft, Apple, Netscape and other websites.

If you use a multimedia file type that is not supported by standard browsers, you should include a link to a website for download of the relevant component. For example, if you provide a *Real Audio* source (*see* **Audio**, *below*), you should include a link to the Real website to allow visitors to download the necessary *RealPlayer* software.

Multimedia components available in Internet Explorer 5

A typical invitation to download necessary plug-ins

AUDIO

Adding a Windows `.wav` or `.au` file audio recording to a web page is as simple as including it as the target of a hyperlink. For example, to let visitors hear a spoken version of the Gaelic welcome message on the Gairloch site, all that is required is the following HTML code:

```
<a href="fgg.au"><img src="audio.gif" alt="Listen"></a>
```

The image used, `audio.gif`, is a typical little icon used to represent a sound file, and the sound itself is recorded in the `fgg.au` file. The `alt=` entry causes

the word 'Listen' to pop
up on screen if the
visitor's mouse hovers
over the icon. If the visitor
clicks the icon, Windows

will automatically open the *Media Player* application
and replay the sound. *Media Player* offers controls to
stop, start and replay the audio at will.

This all supposes you have the sound that you want to
replay available as an audio file, which is not usually
difficult to achieve. The sound replay system on almost
all PCs is equally capable of recording. A stereo jack
socket is normally provided on the rear panel into
which you can plug a portable cassette player, MiniDisc
player, or any other sound source. Having made the
physical connection, you can then use the Windows
Sound Recorder application (found in **Start/Programs/
Accessories/Multimedia**) to capture sounds played into
the computer as audio files.

Sound Recorder is very simple
to operate, with controls like a
cassette recorder and a volume
display so you can adjust the
input level to suit the signal

(see the application's **Help** file). More sophisticated
recording programs are available as shareware or
commercial applications, but *Sound Recorder* is
adequate for capturing short pre-recorded pieces. On
most PCs you can also record directly from the built-in
CD drive (again, remember copyright).

VIDEO

Including video in your website is just as easy as including audio. The standard Windows *Media Player* (or *QuickTime* on the Apple Mac) will replay several common video file formats. As with the audio example earlier, all that you need is a hyperlink to the video file concerned. When a visitor clicks the link, the player will open and present the video.

Getting suitable video files for your website is not quite so straightforward as with audio, because few PCs include video input facilities as standard. You will need to buy some form of video input card to be installed in the computer, or a unit connected to the **USB** bus or parallel port. Once you have this, just as with audio you can plug in a video source, such as a videocassette player or a camcorder, and record video files with the software supplied. The video recording systems almost always include sound channels to go with the video.

WEBCAMS

A special case of video for websites is the **webcam**. This is the term for a dedicated camera connected to a PC, feeding a more or less regularly updated picture to a web server for presentation on a website. Some webcams are updated quickly enough to show real motion, others have intervals of minutes or hours between updates. There are thousands of webcams on the Web, showing everything from a live view from a taxi cab in New York to a set of cameras watching Loch Ness for signs of the monster!

It might sound as if a lot of technology and skill would be needed to set up a webcam, but in fact it is very straightforward. You will need the hardware – a video camera and interface to the computer – but sets are available along with all the necessary software for well under

The image updates every 120 seconds.

£100. The software simply generates GIF or JPEG files from the camera for inclusion in a web page, just like any other graphic. The main complication is that, in order to update the picture, your computer must upload a fresh image file to your web server. So, unless you have a free permanent Internet connection (for example, at a college), you are likely to want to limit the update frequency to minimize your connection charges.

VIRTUAL REALITY

A very simple way to present a scene interactively is to create 'virtual reality' files which allow visitors to control their own gaze or movement. There are some very advanced, computer-generated 3D virtual reality systems, but on a much simpler scale you can stitch together several digital photos to form a large panorama that can be panned from side to side, zoomed in and out, and tilted up and down by the visitor. This requires a suitable **Virtual Reality Mark-up Language (VRML)** plug-in installed to view the files. There are several shareware and retail utilities, with corresponding free viewers available for constructing and viewing VRML files.

ANIMATIONS

Simple web animations provided by **animated GIF** files are ideal for adding life to a page, without any coding complications – the file is handled like any simple bitmap image. They are particularly good for drawing attention to small icons, with a simple effect like a little 'twinkle' on a logo, but beware of overusing these effects – they can be very distracting and annoying in extreme cases.

The GIF format can hold multiple bitmap images in one file, along with timing information to control the sequential display of the bitmaps. This allows simple animation to be presented in something like an electronic version of a flip book. Of course, as more frames are added to the file its size grows, though GIF is capable of storing just the changes from frame to frame.

There are many software packages dedicated to the creation of animated GIFs, including Microsoft's *GIF Animator* (available free at www.microsoft.com/ imagecomposer). A cut-down version of *Corel Xara*, *Xara Webster 2,* can create, edit and optimize animated GIFs, with full control over frame order and timing.

Ulead's *Web Razor Pro* has two applications for making animated GIFs – one for general purpose effects, the other dedicated to animated 3D text and logos – as well as the optimization module mentioned earlier.

Far more sophisticated animations can be created with more advanced authoring tools. The two most popular formats for the Web are *Macromedia Shockwave* and *Flash*. They require specific plug-ins to be installed, but these are shipped as standard with *Internet Explorer 5*, so many people have them without needing to make a large download. Otherwise the plug-ins can be downloaded from www.macromedia.com, which is also a good site to visit to take a look at the possibilities offered by these systems. Be warned, however, the software to create them is not cheap, and the files can be large and slow if you get carried away by their abilities!

In-page animations can also be created with one of the programming languages directly supported by browsers, such as **Java applets** or **JavaScript**. These automatically download a small computer program online to the browser as part of a web page, and this is executed on the visitor's own PC to generate the required effects on the page. These mini-applications can provide advanced user interaction and can change the information on a page instantly without any further downloading, but programming skills are required to create them. Modules of pre-written code are available in authoring tools and from other websites to create standard effects such as 'mouse rollovers', which change the look of an element on the page as the pointer passes over it.

TABLES

From the layout point of view, a big step forward occurred in HTML 3.2 with the introduction of tables (you'll see why later). Before this, tables could be laid out only with complex and unreliable combinations of fixed-pitch typeface (*Courier*) and spaces – no better than the facilities of early wordprocessors and typewriters. HTML nowadays can code remarkably complex table layouts with text mark-up tags of the sort that you have already seen for simple text layout. Here is a very simple table giving details of railway times:

| Inverness | 10:45 | 18:00 |
| Achnasheen | 11:58 | 19:14 |

This would be coded in HTML as:

```
<table border="1" cellpadding="2" cellspacing="0">
    <tr>
        <td>Inverness</td>
        <td>1045</td>
        <td>1800</td>
    </tr>
    <tr>
        <td>Achnasheen</td>
        <td>1158</td>
        <td>1914</td>
    </tr>
</table>
```

You shouldn't find this very hard to follow. The **table** tag simply marks the start and end of the table (the border and cell attributes of the tag control the thickness of the divider lines and the space around the cells). The `tr` tag marks out each new row of the table and the `td` tag marks out each new cell within the row, and you can see how easy it is to create a simple table. Additional tags allow for joining cells together to span rows or columns, and for providing captions and headings.

In larger or less regular tables the coding can become lengthy and complex, and in practice it is much easier to use the table creation facilities built into an authoring tool. *FrontPage Express* has a table creation button that provides a quick, interactive way to specify a new table that will be familiar to users of *Microsoft Word*.

You may think that tables are rather ordinary to have been described as 'a big step forward', but we have only scratched the surface of them here. Each cell of a table acts as a container, with most of the same abilities as a full page – it can have a background colour or image, can contain another 'nested' table, and can control the alignment of its contents.

This opens up a terrific range of possibilities for page layout, where the whole page may be composed of tables within tables – often with invisible borders – in order to achieve complex designs, but these are often better done using the more advanced **cascading style sheets** system.

PULLING THE CROWDS

Having created your website and successfully uploaded it, you could be forgiven for thinking the job is done. But a website with no visitors is as much use as a magazine with no readers! Unless you are lucky enough to be publishing a website strictly for a 'captive' audience (for example, restricted to members of a particular club or company), you now need to promote the site and marshal a steady stream of visitors.

Fortunately, promoting your site worldwide need not cost anything in cash terms. You *can* spend money to promote it with online or traditional advertising, but many of the most effective methods of promotion are entirely free. What you *do* need is time, effort and knowledge of how to go about it. Only you can provide the time and effort, but this chapter will tell you how to apply yourself for best effect.

Search engines

On most websites, more than 80% of new visitors arrive as a result of a query to a **search engine** such as *AltaVista* or *HotBot*. From your own web browsing experience, you will know why this is – where do you go when you are surfing the Web for sites about a new topic? To a search engine, of course.

In a search engine, users enter a keyword or phrase about a topic of interest, then click **Search** and, as if by magic, back comes a list of links to sites associated with those words. Your immediate goal is to make sure that, when potential visitors are looking for sites on the same topic as yours, the search engine lists your pages as near to the top of the pile of search results as possible.

HOW DO SEARCH ENGINES WORK?

If you want to make sure that potential visitors find your site, it will help you to know a little about how search engines work. They do not wait until a particular query is entered before searching the Web for matching sites – that would mean months of waiting before the query could be answered. In fact, part of the search engine system spends day and night continuously searching all the sites it can find (known as 'web crawling'), and forming an index of the words and phrases occurring on those sites. Then, when it receives a query, it can simply look up the keywords in its index, and send back a list of matching web page URLs and titles, and either a brief description or just the first few words from each page.

Nowadays, there are simply too many websites, with too much information on them, for full-text searching to be the most efficient way to index the Web. So there's an improved method in which site designers choose the particular keywords they believe are most relevant to their pages, and can also specify separate page descriptions for the search engine to present in the results list. Most search engines will rank the results for pages found by keyword matches higher in the results list than they rank those found by full text searches. Some search engines will include only those web pages that provide formal keywords and description.

Meaningful page titles and good descriptions of your pages are also important once your site has been identified by keyword. If you have provided a description, the search engine will present this in the results list along with your page title and URL, so it is important to make the description both informative and inviting. The keywords are important to get your site into the top results in a search list, but after that it's down to the description to persuade visitors to choose your particular page from the list.

CHOOSING KEYWORDS

To pick the best keywords for your site, ask yourself what search words or phrases your target visitors are likely to enter when they are searching for something about the subject of your site. The better you can match your keywords to the likely search terms, the more often your pages will turn up in the search engine results.

For the best coverage, your keywords should be a mixture of the general ('scotland', 'highlands') and the specific ('gairloch'). You can also use phrases that seem likely to be used as search items ('walking in scotland'), but don't rely only on these, because the chances of other people picking your exact phrases could be quite low. You might also want to include common misspellings, alternate forms or even foreign spellings of your keywords ('schottland, gair loch') if you think these are likely entries.

ENTERING KEYWORDS AND DESCRIPTIONS

Having chosen suitable keywords and descriptions, what do you do with them? There are dozens of major search engines on the Web, and millions of pages, so it's completely impractical for every webmaster to submit the information directly to every search engine. This problem is solved by the inclusion of special tags in your web pages, called **meta tags**. Any search engine wishing to index your pages will look at each page and extract the keyword and description information directly from the meta tag information in the file. So you need only set up the information once in the page for all search engines to use it.

Meta tag is a term for HTML tags that do not form part of the page content themselves, but contain information about the page. These tags appear in the header portion of a web page and can be used as handy places to keep all sorts of information about the page. Each meta tag consists of a HTML tag called `<META>` plus a pair of properties giving a name for each type of information and the contents of that item. An example will make this clearer.

For the sample Gairloch site we might choose keywords including 'gairloch', 'scotland' and 'highlands', and a description based on the one that was used on the home page. To enter these in the page HTML you would insert the following:

```
<meta name="keywords" content="gairloch,
scotland, highlands">
```

```
<meta name="description" content="Find out all
about the beautiful area of Gairloch in Wester
Ross, Scotland">
```

Note that capital letters are unimportant in keywords, so you may as well enter everything in lowercase. You can type these keywords directly in the HTML, on lines between the <HEAD> and the </HEAD> tags, or your authoring package may have facilities to enter them via a dialogue box. An alternative is to use one of the free **meta tag builders** available on the Web, such as the one at webpromote.com, which is easy to use.

In *FrontPage Express*, meta tags are entered through the **File**, **Page properties** dialogue. Go to the **Custom** tab and in the **User** variables panel you will see that *FrontPage Express* has already entered itself as the 'generator' of the

page. This is where you can add the keywords and description variables, with whatever content you want.

SUBMITTING TO A SEARCH

You might be wondering how a search engine knows your site is there on the Web to be indexed. One way, which requires no action from you, is for it to come across your site from a link on another site during a web crawl, just as any visitor might. This is not a very effective way for a new site to be found, unless you have persuaded a lot of other sites to link to yours (*see* **Link exchanges**, *page 174*). A more direct method is to use the **submit** option provided by most search engines. This involves filling in a short online form to register the URL of your site with the search engine, which will add it to the list of sites to be indexed in the next few days.

It is reckoned that 99% of people who turn to the Web for information use less than 10 of the top search engines, so make your submissions to the major sites first. These

include *Alta Vista, Excite, HotBot, InfoSeek, MSN, Netscape Netcenter, Yahoo!* and *Lycos*. You will find a submission option on the main pages of each of these. Make sure that you have set up your keywords and descriptions before doing this, as otherwise most search engines will ignore your submission.

As there are so many search engines, and it could be a full-time occupation keeping your submissions up to date with all of them, a number of specialist **submission engines** will send your details to a wide range of sites automatically. They generally charge for the service, but they often offer a free trial with a limited number of submissions (*see* **How am I doing?**, *opposite*). If the content of your site is specifically national in content, or you are particularly looking for visitors from one country, then you could concentrate your efforts on the search engines that people use when they are looking for

UK-SPECIFIC SEARCH ENGINES

These search engines and directories specialize in sites with predominantly UK content:

BritIndex – www.britindex.co.uk

Excite UK Edition – www.excite.co.uk

G.O.D. – www.god.co.uk

Global Business Centre –
www.euromktg.com/gbc/en.html

Infoseek UK Plus – www.ukplus.com

Lifestyle.UK – www.lifestyle.co.uk

Lycos UK – www.lycos.co.uk

Mug-O-Milk – www.mugomilk.freeserve.co.uk

UK Directory – www.ukdirectory.com

UKIndex – www.ukindex.co.uk/uksearch.html

Yahoo UK – www.yahoo.co.uk

Yell – www.yell.co.uk

Yellowweb – www.yweb.com/adv-en.html

country-specific websites. Several of the big names, such as *Alta Vista*, *MSN* and *Yahoo!*, have regional variants, and there are many less well-known regional search engines.

HOW AM I DOING?

You should regularly review how well your site is faring in the search engines by submitting sample queries and seeing who comes top of the pile. If your site deals with a popular topic, you may well find that you need to make frequent revisions to keywords to maintain your position. It can take a lot of time to check out your site across many search engines, but there are some very useful tools available.

One of the most advanced tools is *TopDog*, which sends automated queries using your choice of keywords to over 180 search engines. When the results come back a few minutes later, it presents detailed reports of your site's ranking at each engine, so that you can take action (or sit back and congratulate yourself!). *TopDog* also has a powerful submission system that can automatically submit or resubmit your site if its rank falls below a preset level. You can download a free trial of *TopDog* that works with five search engines at a time (www. topdog.com).

Link exchanges

If there are other websites on topics related to yours, your target audiences will overlap and you could benefit from having **reciprocal links** with them. This involves nothing more than agreeing with the operator of the other site that you will each include a link to the other in an appropriate place (for example, on your links page). Most private website operators are happy to do this, as it generally increases the number of visitors all round and you are unlikely to be in direct commercial competition. The process is made easier if you prepare standard pieces of text, and perhaps a graphical button for your site, which you can mail out to other webmasters.

These agreements are usually informal, involving nothing more than an exchange of e-mails suggesting and agreeing to the links. There are also some organized link-exchanging services, and a particularly good one is *bCentral Banner Exchange* – formerly *LinkExchange* – (www.bcentral.com). This is one of many features on Microsoft's *bCentral* site, which also offers an excellent newsletter digest for web designers. It is well worth looking at if you are serious about boosting your site's visitor count.

Your website might also fall into an area of interest covered by a 'web ring', which offers a means for each website in a co-operating group to provide a link to another member of the group. That member will, in turn, have a link to another. This means that, with no

bCentral web marketing from Microsoft

more than one or two links on your pages, your visitors can depart on a merry crawl around other sites on the same topic, and fresh visitors will come to your site from other members of the ring. Some rings offer a random button that doesn't move visitors on to a specific next site in the ring but can jump to any member at random.

A typical web ring banner

Talk your way to the top

Well, not literally, but take every reasonable opportunity to mention your site in e-mails, letters, bulletin board and newsgroup postings, and so on. If your e-mail program lets you add a standard 'signature' to each outgoing message, make sure you use it to draw attention to your site. However, beware of upsetting people with blatant advertising. Most operators of mailing lists and newsgroups regard a four-line signature (including your name) as a reasonable thing, so you might sign yourself with a name and company, the title and URL of your website, plus a one-line description or slogan for your site.

If there are self-help newsgroups or bulletin boards dealing with topics covered by your site, try to join in and provide helpful and informative replies. This will establish your knowledge of the topic and general willingness to contribute to the online community, and is a much more effective way to encourage incidental visitors to your site than direct plugs. Remember also that for each person who actively writes to such services there are usually dozens, maybe hundreds, of others who are just reading (you might hear them referred to as 'lurkers').

Repeat business

Of course, as well as pulling in new visitors, you should do all you can to encourage repeat visits from people who have already found you once. The single most effective way to encourage repeat visits is to pack your site with top-quality interesting, entertaining and useful material. Okay, easier said than done, but this is the direction in which you should aim. If you don't have the resources to create a huge top-quality site, try to create a small one. Don't be tempted to put up mediocre or rehashed information just because it's easy. People may visit once, but they won't return.

Having created a good site, keep it up to date. If visitors return to your site after a few weeks and see no change, they are unlikely ever to come back. That doesn't mean reworking every page frequently. It might only mean changing one or two pages a month and refreshing the home page. It's also worth making the design of the home page show explicitly that it is subject to change (with a 'What's new' headline and a 'Last updated' footer, for example). *See also* **Maintaining your site**, *page 178.*

MAINTAINING YOUR SITE

It is all too easy to publish a site and then let it lie 'out of sight, out of mind', but that is not the way to achieve your objectives for the site. If you take pride in keeping your pages well maintained, it will show in the level of repeat visits. This means keeping the content up to date, checking and correcting links to other sites and, whenever possible, regularly improving and extending the site.

A side benefit of updating is that, when people search the Internet using a **search engine**, they are usually shown a 'last updated' caption against each page found, which is based on the date of the page file itself. If you always reload your home page whenever you make any changes to the site, visitors will know it is being actively maintained. An experienced search engine user may even specify date ranges of interest, and would simply not find your pages unless you took care to update them regularly (*see* **Search engines**, *page 167*).

Make sure that there is a clear contact address on the website for you as its 'webmaster', so that visitors can send in problem reports, suggestions and even compliments. When you receive a problem report, don't treat it as a complaint – you should be pleased that someone has made the effort to let you know of an easy way to make the site better. Take the time to mail a short thank-you note to the writer (you can keep a 'standard letter' ready in your e-mail to make this easier), and then make sure you deal with the problem promptly and professionally.

Some people subscribe to automated site watch services, which alert them by e-mail when a website changes. If they are interested in your site, they may have set up a watch on its home page. By making sure that your home page is always updated when anything in the rest of the site changes, you will increase the chances of these people returning to your page.

Setting up a site watch

Updating the site

If your site is not a very busy one, and it is not your full-time job to look after it, try to settle on a routine for dealing with minor changes regularly, perhaps once a week. You can keep a note of any problems reported or that you have observed during the week, and probably fix them all in a few minutes. The easiest way to maintain a modest site is to keep the original files in place on your local PC, even after you have uploaded the site. That way, you can check and modify files offline before transferring all the updates in one brief online operation.

Unless your website is based on an online authoring system (*see* **Tools of the trade**, *page 29*), you should resist the temptation to use any online editing facilities offered by your authoring software. It is much easier to keep track of things if you have a complete local reference copy of your site, and make any changes there. Occasionally, someone may report a problem that is only apparent online and not on your local copy (for example, as a result of a link that refers mistakenly to a local file on your PC). If you come across this sort of problem, use your browser to identify the cause online, but then make the corrections to your offline copy and reload the relevant files to the server.

Watching the traffic

You can gain a useful insight into improving the success of your site by looking at its visitor statistics. Many web server hosts provide usage logs in files automatically deposited in one of your server directories (typically called something like `/logs/access.log`). These are usually huge data files that need some analysis or interpretation to be really useful. Many of the better web hosting services will automatically process these files into useful charts and tables in web pages that you can browse. Make the most of these to find out:

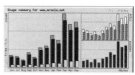

- how many visitors your site receives and when
- where your visitors are coming from
- which files are missing or wrongly called for
- which browsers your visitors are using

You can use these figures to see how well you are doing generally, to spot trends and, more importantly, to see what you could improve. You will see things like 'File not found' errors where you have removed a page that was linked from another website, so you can ask the other site to update the link. You can also keep an eye on the pattern of visits from search engines to see where you should be making new URL submissions (*see* **Pulling the crowds**, *page 166*).

If your web host does not provide analysis, or you want to look more closely, you can choose from a selection of traffic analysis tools. Some of these are cheap, or free in return for a banner or logo on your site. You can find a range of tools at reallybig.com/stats.shtml. When you are selecting traffic log analysis tools, it is vital to confirm that the software is compatible with your server. Most of the better tools can handle all the popular web server log file formats.

VISITOR COUNTERS

You may want to put a 'hit counter' on your home page. This will tell you how many visitors it has had, and you can set it up to display the figures online. It may be best to avoid this until the site has built up a reasonable number of hits (some cheat, and start the counter at a healthy figure!). The value of a visible counter is hard to assess, but many people like them.

A counter needs a small amount of script language or support from the server to maintain and display the counts, but there are many sites offering links to free counter services – find some by doing a web search on 'visitor counters', or take a look at the list on reallybig.com/counters.shtml. If you want to use the counter script that is built into *FrontPage Express*, your web server must support *FrontPage Extensions* – ask the server provider if this can be set up (sometimes there is a charge).

Counter styles

Onward and upward

So now you have a website, you know how to monitor its use and how to change it. You've joined the thousands of web publishers who have discovered the thrill of being able to publish worldwide from their own home or office.

Make the most of the freedom to alter your website to adapt to the changing world, to utilize new Web techniques and software, and to meet the ever-changing needs of your visitors.

You'll find that hardly a day goes by without your thinking of some way to improve the site, or of somewhere new to promote it, or even of a topic for a completely new website. Go for it!

Glossary

absolute file reference A reference including the drive or directory path, which changes if the file's directory is moved.

Adobe Acrobat Software to create compressed Portable Document Format (**PDF**) files.

animated GIF Multiple images in **GIF** files that are cycled to produce simple animation.

anti-aliasing Filling in edges of irregular shapes with shading to give a smoother look.

applet A small computer program, operating as a plug-in or control in a web page.

AU, **AVI** Windows-supported formats for audio and audiovisual files.

authoring tool Software to help create web pages and sites.

banner ad Advertisement bars or buttons on web pages.

bevel Shading on graphic edges, giving a look of depth.

bitmap An image composed of a rectangular grid of coloured dots (pixels).

bookmark Reference to a specifically marked spot within a web page. Also a Netscape term for **Favorites**.

broken link A **hyperlink** that points to a **target** that no longer exists, or has moved.

browser *See* **web browser**.

browser-safe colours A **colour palette** of 216 unique colours that can be faithfully reproduced by a **browser**.

bullets Graphical marks beside each item in a list. May be used on web pages as **hyperlinks**.

cache Temporary storage area on your disk, used to speed up repeated access to popular web pages. *See also* **temporary Internet files**.

cascading style sheets (**CSS**) A mark-up system allowing text styles of a web page to be defined separately from its structure and content.

CGI Common Gateway Interface – programming system used on **web servers** to automate response forms, image maps, guestbooks and other processes.

colour palette The full set of display colours available for use. Common palettes include 24-bit colour ('true colour', or 16.7 million colours), and 8-bit colour (256-colour).

compression Processing files to reduce their size without unacceptable loss of information. **Lossless** methods recover all the original data perfectly; **lossy** methods do not.

cookie A small data file stored on your computer by a **web server**, helping it identify you and your data.

digital camera An electronic camera that stores pictures as digital image files, not on film.

dithering Creating intermediate shades by finely mixing colours from the available palette.

domain name The definitive registered name for a website or service.

download Copy a file from a **web server** to your computer.

drop shadows Graphic shading designed to make objects stand out from a page.

Dynamic HTML (**DHTML**) Enhanced **HTML** for programmed changes to page design without reloading.

eye candy Embellishments to make a site more attractive.

Favorites The **Internet Explorer** term for a collection of web links saved for easy return visits.

font embedding A system for including font information within a web page.

frames Panels within a browser display, where **hyperlinks** in one panel may control the page displayed in another.

FrontPage Popular web authoring software. Also available in a simpler free version, *FrontPage Express.*

FTP File Transfer Protocol – the standard method of retrieving files from a computer on the Internet.

GIF Graphics Interchange Format – a widely used graphics file format, developed by CompuServe. Also capable of holding short animated sequences of frames.

guestbook The website equivalent of a conventional guest book, where visitors can leave comments.

history files Files storing details of pages visited.

home page The main entry page for a website. Also the default start page shown by a **web browser.**

hotspot Any spot on a web page that does something when clicked or pointed to.

HTML Hypertext Markup Language – the **mark-up** language used for coding all web pages.

HTTP HyperText Transport Protocol – the method used for sending web pages via the Internet.

hyperlink A reference from one web page to another, which can be 'followed' by a web browser. Links may be 'internal' to a page within the same site, or 'external' to other sites.

image map A web graphic that links to various other locations, according to where on the image you click.

Internet Explorer   The **web browser** produced by Microsoft. Currently used for more than 60% of web page visits.

Java, **JavaScript**   Programming languages used for dynamic effects on web pages.

JPEG   A graphics file format widely used on the Internet. Can achieve high compression of photographic images.

link   Shorthand for a **hyperlink**.

local   File or website stored and viewed on the same PC.

Lynx   A text-based browser, very useful for people with visual disabilities.

mark-up   Codes inserted in text to control its appearance, and to handle web page features such as **hyperlinks**.

meta tags   HTML **mark-up** tags containing information about a web page, such as keywords or author's name.

MIDI   A compact file format used for simple system-generated music on web pages.

Netscape Communicator   A complete suite of Internet authoring, browsing, e-mail and collaboration software, including *Netscape Composer*, *Navigator* and *Messenger*.

Netscape Navigator   A very popular **web browser**, especially on Apple computers.

online editors   Web-based **authoring tools** for the direct creation of web pages online.

optimization   Selection of the best data and **compression** settings to achieve the smallest usable file size.

PDF   Portable Document Format – *see* **Adobe Acrobat**.

plug-ins   Add-in software to extend the capability of a **web browser** or other application.

PNG   Portable Network Graphics – a graphics file format intended as a long-term replacement for **GIF**.

proxy server A security device that replaces the direct connection between a PC or network and the Internet to prevent unauthorised access.

RealAudio A popular format for Internet delivery of sound sources in real time.

reciprocal links Matching **hyperlinks** placed on two sites to encourage a flow of visitors between them.

refresh, **reload** Retrieve a fresh, up-to-date copy of a web page in the browser.

relative file reference A file name specified in relation to the position of the referring file.

search engine An Internet service for searching websites for keywords or phrases.

ShockWave A browser plug-in to view animated, interactive material from *Macromedia Director*.

streaming Sending real-time audio or video content over a network, optimized for smooth delivery. *See also* **RealAudio**.

submission engine An automatic system to add new sites for indexing in **search engines**.

SVG A new standard for encoding **vector graphics** on the Web.

tags Mark-up codes inside <angle brackets> in **HTML**.

tags-on-view An **authoring tool** display, which is essentially **WYSIWYG**, but also inserts small markers to show the positions of **mark-up** codes.

temporary Internet files Microsoft's term for files that store the content of recently visited web pages, allowing them to be redisplayed rapidly from **local** storage.

transparency Feature of **GIF** and **PNG** files, allowing the background to show through selected parts of **bitmap** images.

upload To transfer files to a main server or remote site. Used to 'publish' local files to a **web server**.

URL Uniform Resource Locator – addressing scheme used by the Web to identify web pages, files and other resources.

USB Universal Serial Bus – a quick system for interconnecting computers and multiple peripherals. Popular for fast modems, printers and **digital cameras**.

vector graphics Graphics composed of geometric objects, such as lines and polygons.

virtual reality Computer simulation of real or imaginary objects and environments.

VRML Virtual Reality Markup Language – an extension of **HTML** for coding **virtual reality** effects.

web browser Any software application used to navigate and display pages on the Web.

web crawler Software that automatically follows web page links from page to page and site to site, usually for automatic indexing work.

web server A computer that stores web pages and delivers them to browsers on demand.

webcam Video cameras that feed images directly into web pages.

web-safe colours *See* **browser-safe**.

WYSIWYG editors Authoring tools in which the user sees the results during editing approximately as they will be displayed by a browser, rather than seeing mark-up codes and plain text.

INDEX

COLLINS GEM
BABIES
names

COLLINS GEM
BEER

COLLINS GEM
BIRDS

COLLINS GEM
CALORIE
Counter

COLLINS GEM
FACT FILE

COLLINS GEM

COLLINS GEM
FLAGS

COLLINS GEM
Healthy
EATING

COLLINS GEM
QUOTATIONS

COLLINS GEM
SAS
Self-Defence

COLLINS GEM
SAS
Survival Guide

COLLINS GEM
SEASHORE

COLLINS GEM
TREES

COLLINS GEM
Understanding
DREAMS

COLLINS GEM
WILD
flowers

COLLINS GEM
WINE
dictionary